LEGAL AND ILLICIT DRUG USE

LEGAL AND ILLICIT DRUG USE

Acute Reactions of Emergency-Room Populations

James A. Inciardi
Duane C. McBride
Anne E. Pottieger
Brian R. Russe
Harvey A. Siegal

PRAEGER PUBLISHERS
Praeger Special Studies

New York • London • Sydney • Toronto

Library of Congress Cataloging in Publication Data

Main entry under title:

Legal and illicit drug use.

    Bibliography: p.
    Includes index.
    1. Medication abuse--United States. 2. Drugs
--Side effects. 3. Alcoholism--United States.
4. Hospitals--United States--Emergency service.
5. Drug abuse surveys--United States.
6. Dade Co., Fla.--Statistics, Medical.
I. Inciardi, James A.
RM146.5.L43   614.3'5   78-19743

ISBN 0-03-046701-2

The data used in the preparation of this material were obtained with the support of DHEW Grant H81DA0880 from the National Institute on Drug Abuse to the Division of Addiction Sciences, Department of Psychiatry, University of Miami School of Medicine, 1972–76.

PRAEGER PUBLISHERS
PRAEGER SPECIAL STUDIES
383 Madison Avenue, New York, N.Y. 10017, U.S.A.

Published in the United States of America in 1978
by Praeger Publishers,
A Division of Holt, Rinehart and Winston, CBS, Inc.

89   038   987654321

ACKNOWLEDGMENTS

The total number of debts one incurs during research investigations is surprisingly large, especially when project efforts endure over a period of years. Without question, adequate acknowledgment is not always possible, for there are many whose contributions are difficult to fully measure, or in some cases, do not come to one's attention. Nevertheless, our thanks must be extended to all those who participated in the project, from its inception to its final days, and to the many who were never formally associated with the research, but without whom our endeavor might not have reached its fullest completion.

Special thanks must be extended to Carl D. Chambers for his initial conception of the project, to David M. Petersen for his labor in making it operational, and to L. Thomas Carroll and James Sussex for their strong support throughout its full duration. For their efforts and cooperation in providing access to the local drug treatment delivery network, we are indebted to Charles Lincoln and the entire staff of the Metropolitan Dade County Comprehensive Drug Program, to the medical personnel at Jackson Memorial Hospital, and to Ronald Wright of the Dade County Medical Examiner's Office.

Our data collection and data reduction efforts were sometimes overwhelming, and for their assistance in this behalf we are indebted to Clyde McCoy, Robert Orgaz, Carolyn Williams, Ann L. Russe, Carolyn J. Inciardi, Sarah Greenberger, Debbie Surplus, and Joanne Walter.

Finally, thanks are owed to Barry S. Brown, Thomas Voskuhl, Rebecca Ashery, staff of the National Institute on Drug Abuse, and to the many who cannot be named, yet whose cooperation made the study possible.

CONTENTS

LIST OF TABLES

1

INTRODUCTION: THE ACUTE DRUG REACTIONS PROJECT

The use of drugs for the enhancement of pleasure or perfor-
mance has been viewed within a problematic context in this country
for the better part of a century. Public concern over drug use first
emerged during the mid-1800s with the widespread availability of
opium and its derivatives in patent medicines, the use of injectable
morphine for the treatment of pain, and the smoking of opium among
the Chinese and avant-garde populations of the nation's coastal
cities. With the introduction of heroin in 1898, a new population of
drug users became apparent, made even more visible with the pas-
sage of the Harrison Act in 1914.* Since that time, a criminal
model of drug use has sought to manage the phenomenon of drug
taking through legislation and repression, while a medical model
of drug use has sought to deal with drug taking within a rehabilita-
tive context (see Inciardi 1974b).

Current approaches to the treatment of drug use embrace a
wide variety of techniques, and while a number of these modalities
have clearly demonstrated success with significant numbers of
substance abusers, research has demonstrated that an even larger
population has not reflected measurable benefits from these approaches, and that vast numbers of drug-involved individuals may
not be coming to the attention of the formal human-service delivery
network. Furthermore, it has been hypothesized that a number of
treatment-program failures may have occurred as a result of
treatment intervention occurring either too late in an individual's
substance-abuse career, or at a time when the user is unmotivated
for treatment.

---

*This act defined possession of narcotics as illegal.

1

THE INITIAL PROJECT

Within this context an Acute Drug Reactions Project (ADRP) was initiated at the University of Miami's School of Medicine in May 1972 to determine the extent to which the hospital emergency room might be utilized for the identification and analysis of drug-abuse phenomena. More specifically, it was anticipated that the project would serve as a mechanism for defining the parameters of any substance-abusing populations coming to the attention of emergency-room medical personnel, for examining the nature of the drug use resulting in emergency-room appearances, for determining whether the kinds of drugs abused and the characteristics of these populations were changing over time, and for indicating what proportion of these drug-emergency patients were not coming to the attention of the local drug-treatment delivery system. In addition, a hypothesis investigated was that patients suffering from drug-related physical and/or psychological crises and seeking treatment at emergency-room facilities would be more receptive to therapeutic treatment alternatives during the crisis situation than either prior to the onset of the crisis, or subsequent to the resolution of the crisis.

The project was based at Jackson Memorial Hospital, a facility having the fourth largest emergency room in the United States and processing approximately 500 persons per day. Jackson Memorial is also the teaching hospital for the University of Miami's School of Medicine, and represents the only public hospital serving greater Dade County, Florida. Hospital records for a six-month period (May through November 1971) were drawn for 450 drug-related emergency-room visits in an effort to furnish the baseline information necessary for implementation of the Acute Drug Reactions Project. It was found that a third of these cases were the result of illicit-substance use and two-thirds were from legally manufactured and distributed substances. Drug-emergency patients were from various age, sex, racial, and ethnic groups, and, with the exception of obvious psychiatric disorders treated at inpatient or outpatient psychiatric facilities, they were not provided post-emergency or posthospital services relative to their recent drug experience. Furthermore, no followup was attempted by any social service agency in the area. As such, the patients who came to the hospital with drug-induced problems were simply medically treated and then discharged. A later examination of medical records also showed many of the drug-abusing patients to be chronic repeaters at Jackson Memorial Hospital's emergency room. As an obviously needed alternative to facilities that provide only crisis medical treatment, a federal grant for "Post-Emergency Services for Acute

Drug Reactions Cases" was provided to study the possibilities for
offering referral services to emergency drug patients.

 With medical records providing names, addresses, and pertinent medical and substance-use information on all patients using
the emergency-room facilities for drug reactions, 200 subjects, of
which 100 had used illicit substances and 100 had used licit substances, were randomly selected to participate in an extended interview. The interview, conducted in the home of the subject, was
designed to provide the demographic data typically not available in
the hospital records. Subjects were also queried as to their use of
alcohol and other drugs, including both prescription and illicit substances, and as to the length and frequency of use. Knowledge as
to the type of drug user utilizing the emergency-room facilities was
deemed a necessary forerunner to the establishment of a referral
system which could be a viable research project and a practical
therapeutic endeavor. In addition, by assessing the target population's perceptions as to appropriate and desirable types of service
agencies, the compilation of a referral list used for that particular
population could be firmly and realistically based.

 As the project progressed, it was realized that the emergency
room presented a larger and more diverse population of drug abusers than anticipated, and that little was known regarding the extent
of acute drug reactions, the kinds of drugs abused that resulted in
emergency treatment, and the characteristics of the population receiving such emergency care. In 1975, attempts were made to expand the project so as to develop a broad epidemiological data base
on the drug-emergency phenomena in Miami, and to contrast these
phenomena with those of alternative urban areas. This development
of a broader data base was attempted through the development of a
consortium which would include the then federally funded polydrug
projects.

THE POLYDRUG PROJECTS

 In 1973, the National Institute on Drug Abuse funded 13 polydrug projects across the nation. Their primary focus was on those
populations who used a variety of substances in combination with
one another and often came to local hospital emergency rooms seeking help for drug-related problems. Prior to this time, the federal
government had funded programs to treat persons whose primary
drug of abuse was heroin. These were the "streetwise" drug users
described by Wesson, Smith, and Lerner (1975). The term "polydrug" became widely publicized through these federal polydrug research and demonstration projects, which were placed in major

cities reported by the Drug Abuse Warning Network (DAWN) as having extensive nonopiate drug-abuse problems. These included Boston, New York, Minneapolis, Philadelphia, Richmond, Detroit, Denver, Houston, Seattle, San Francisco, Durham, and San Diego. The projects were designed to provide basic data about polydrug-abusing populations; develop a knowledgeable cadre of nonopiate treatment experts; and develop and define the most effective therapeutic techniques, particularly in the area of effective detoxification for mixed addictions.

By mid-1973, preliminary findings from the polydrug projects suggested that the users involved appeared to be a subpopulation of the opiate users generally found in the federally funded treatment programs. In terms of social functioning, the polydrug users showed great similarity to the previously reported opiate-using clients. These similarities centered on arrest rates, employment, occupational level, education, and prior treatment histories (Benvenuto and Bourne 1975). The Boston polydrug project found little difference between the polydrug users and the opiate users in terms of sex, age, prior drug treatment histories, prior psychiatric treatment histories, prior occurrence of imprisonment, and age of initial drug use. However, there were noticeable differences between the two populations in terms of ethnicity, divorce rates, education, the number of drugs used, and their level of depression (Raynes, Patch, and Cohen 1975).

The San Diego and Detroit polydrug projects both found that polydrug users were more neuropsychologically impaired than comparative groups of non-drug-using patients. After a five-hour battery of psychological tests was administered to all subjects, results indicated that the majority of the polydrug users' test means lay in an impaired range (Judd and Grant 1975; Adams et al. 1975). The Denver polydrug project found that polydrug users appeared to be a heterogeneous group, and their demographic characteristics were similar to those found in the general population of Colorado. The project also found that the users were primarily white males with a median age of 27.8 years. Also, half of the polydrug users had been arrested within the previous two years (Kirby and Berry 1975).

Among the noteworthy findings of the polydrug projects was the indication that there was no overwhelming demand for treatment by the targeted users. However, the projects estimated that approximately 2.5 million persons in the United States had nonopiate drug-related problems. In addition, the users appeared to be members of the middle class involved in self-medication.

THE STRUCTURING OF A CONSORTIUM

Projects established during the polydrug funding era were contacted and invited to Miami for a preliminary conference to discuss the goals of a national acute drug reactions study. Of the six projects contacted (Detroit, Denver, San Francisco, Houston, New York, and Washington, D.C.), Denver, Houston, and New York expressed an interest in forming a consortium and applying for funding.

The Houston, Denver, and New York projects were set up prior to the establishment of the consortium as polydrug collection centers and were, therefore, structured somewhat differently from the Miami project. In an effort to mitigate these differences, uniform data collection instruments were designed in consultation with these other centers (see Forms A and B in the Appendix), and these instruments were implemented during mid-1975. As 1975 drew to a close, however, funding difficulties in New York and Houston resulted in incomplete data collection, and the two cities were necessarily excluded from further participation. The data collection in Denver, however, persisted throughout the research.

Denver was able to rapidly reorient its polydrug project to the needs and goals of the consortium and began data collection in July of 1975. The rapid retooling and the existence of a viable and active system within Denver General Hospital to locate drug-involved patients gave Denver an extensive data base on drug users. Hospital wards and the outpatient department as well as the medical emergency room became sites at which drug-involved subjects were located. Until April 1976, both Denver and Miami maintained ongoing emergency data collection with the standardized intake forms. Simultaneously, the Miami Acute Drug Reactions Project expanded its data collection efforts for the purpose of developing a wide-ranging epidemiological base on acute drug reactions.

DATA PRESENTATION

During the full term of the Acute Drug Reactions Project, a variety of epidemiological, demographic, social, and followup data were collected in order to describe the general phenomena of drug and alcohol emergencies. The information gathered was organized for analysis into the data bases described in Table 1.1. As the table indicates, the chapter organization of this book is neither chronological nor based on the geographic location of the data sources.

TABLE 1.1

Data Bases Used in This Book

Data Type and Source	Substance Involved	All or Sample	Number	Period	Chapter of Discussion
Intake information from					
Jackson Memorial Hospital	Drugs	All	11,287	1/72–12/76	2, 3
Jackson Memorial Hospital	Alcohol	All	5,004	7/75–12/76	6
12 private hospitals	Drugs	All	1,470	1/75–12/75	3
Detailed interviews at					
Jackson Memorial Hospital	Drugs	Sample	309	8/75–4/76	4, 5, 6
Jackson Memorial Hospital	Alcohol	Sample	217	8/75–4/76	6
Dade County Comprehensive Drug Program	Drugs	All	1,302	1/74–6/74	5
Denver General Hospital	Drugs	Sample	527	7/75–4/76	4, 6
Denver General Hospital	Alcohol	Sample	478	7/75–4/76	6
Referral followup studies[a] of					
Pre–ADRP medical staff referrals	Heroin	Sample	132	1972	7
ADRP Phase I (active vs. passive)	Drugs	5 samples	92	1972–73	7
ADRP Phase II	Both[b]	Samples	61	3/76–4/76	7
Dade County Medical Examiner					
Substance–related accidents	Both[b]	All	1,078	1/56–12/75	8
All suicides	Both[b]	All	4,018	1/56–12/75	8

[a] All at Jackson Memorial Hospital; ADRP = Acute Drug Reactions Project.
[b] Both drugs and alcohol.
Source: Compiled by the authors.

Rather, as detailed below, the organization of this book is in terms of the logic of the project plus the nature of the information secured from each data source.

Chapter 2 reports basic epidemiological data on the 11,287 patients admitted to Jackson Memorial Hospital during 1972-76 for adverse reactions to drugs, exclusive of alcohol. A significant portion of the analysis is devoted to changes over time in the particular drugs involved in these emergencies, and the changes in the characteristics of the drug-emergency patients having problems with particular kinds of drugs. The same basic data are used again in Chapter 3, but presented in terms of the differences between the Jackson Memorial patients and drug-emergency patients who appeared at the private hospitals in Dade County during 1975. The data collection instrument used for both these populations appears in the Appendix to this book (Form A).

Chapters 4 and 5 focus on more detailed information obtained from a sample of the Jackson Memorial drug-emergency patients discussed in Chapters 2 and 3. Extensive interviews were done with this sample, using the data collection instrument reproduced as Form B in the Appendix. In Chapter 4, the Jackson Memorial patients are compared with clients of the Dade County Comprehensive Drug Program, who were interviewed using a similar set of questions.

Chapter 6 introduces the subject of adverse reactions to alcohol. Baseline data from all 5,004 Jackson Memorial alcohol-emergency cases seen between July 1975 and December 1976 are provided (based on the same instrument [Form A] as that used for the drug-emergency cases), followed by an in-depth analysis of a sample of these same patients, compared to a sample of alcohol-reaction patients interviewed at Denver General Hospital. Chapter 6 is analogous to the information on drug-emergency patients discussed in Chapters 2 and 4, and uses the same data collection instruments (Forms A and B).

Chapter 7 is a description of several experiments in referring emergency-room patients (both drug and alcohol) to community treatment agencies, as well as a presentation of field followup data on these patients.

To round out the epidemiological data on drug and alcohol emergencies, Chapter 8 offers an analysis of substance-related deaths for the 20-year period beginning January 1, 1956. The data collection instrument for this segment of the project also appears in the Appendix (Form C).

Finally, Chapter 9 provides a summary of the project, including implications of the study and suggestions for further research.

2

THE INCIDENCE OF ACUTE DRUG
REACTIONS AT A HOSPITAL EMERGENCY
ROOM, 1972-76

Medical files maintained within a major hospital emergency room represent a source from which a data base can be drawn for describing the populations which come to the attention of emergency rooms for acute/adverse reactions to drugs, and for suggesting the drugs which most often cause such reactions. From these data one can begin to draw some conclusions regarding the nature of drug abuse and medicine misuse within a community, the types of populations having the highest risk of acute/adverse drug reactions, and how these tend to change over time. Miami's Jackson Memorial Hospital was an excellent source for such information, since it treats some 200,000 patients annually in its emergency room, and currently, almost 1.5 percent of these patients receive emergency care for drug-related problems involving accidental overdoses, suicide attempts, addiction syndromes, allergic reactions, and other acute or adverse reactions.

During the five-year period from January 1, 1972 through December 31, 1976, a total of 11,287 patients were treated in the Jackson emergency room for a health or emotional problem related to drugs (excluding alcohol). When a patient is presented at the emergency room, a preliminary medical file is initiated which includes the patient's name, address, age, sex, ethnicity, and the primary substance responsible for admission (if known). In addition to these data, hospital staff provide information on the patient's complaint at admission, clinical status, and ultimate case disposition. While these represent only the most minimal data as to a drug-emergency case, they nevertheless provide a basic data source from which preliminary trends and patterns in drug taking in the hospital's host community can be understood.

DEMOGRAPHIC CHARACTERISTICS
OF PATIENTS

Table 2.1 indicates that among the 11,287 patients treated for
acute/adverse drug reactions at Jackson Memorial Hospital during
the period 1972 through 1976, a slight majority were women. In
terms of race and ethnicity, about 57 percent of the patients were
white, as opposed to 32 percent blacks and 11 percent Hispanics.
These figures indicate that blacks were overrepresented and Hispanics were underrepresented in the emergency-room population, since
the county population is 61 percent white, 15 percent black, and 24
percent Hispanic. The age distribution reported in Table 2.1 shows
the highest incidence of drug emergencies among adolescents and
young adults, with over half the cases being under age 25 and almost
80 percent under age 35. The highest incidence of drug cases fell
within the 18-to-24-year age cohort.

TABLE 2.1

Basic Demographic Characteristics of
11,287 Drug-Emergency Patients, 1972-76

	Number	Percent
Males	5,283	46.8
Females	6,000	53.2
No data	4	<.1
Black	3,616	32.0
Hispanic	1,231	10.9
White	6,396	56.7
No data	44	.4
17 years or less	1,279	11.3
18-24 years	4,568	40.5
25-34 years	3,123	27.7
35-49 years	1,509	13.4
50 years and above	687	6.1
No data	121	1.1
Total	11,287	100.0

Source: Compiled by the authors.

An analysis of these data on a year-to-year basis clearly reflects some emergent trends. First, as indicated below, the number of drug emergencies has steadily increased by some 105 percent over the half-decade period:

Year	Total Cases	Percent Annual Change	
1972	1,354	--	
1973	2,129	+57	
1974	2,397	+13	
1975	2,637	+10	
1976	2,770	+5	105

While it might be argued that these increases may be a reflection of the significant population expansion in the county as a whole, other data would not support this contention. In 1972, for example, the Metropolitan Dade County population was estimated at 1.35 million. By 1976, this figure had increased to 1.45 million, a population change of only +7.4 percent as compared to a drug-emergency-population increase of some 105 percent during the same period.

Table 2.2 suggests additional trends. First, an increasing percentage of drug emergencies were attributable to males. While males represented 43.2 percent of the drug-emergency population in 1972, this figure gradually increased to 50.6 percent in 1976--a proportional increase of 17 percent over the five-year period, with a corresponding decline among females. A less stable pattern emerged with respect to ethnicity. The percentage of whites among drug emergencies declined slightly, from 61.5 percent in 1972 to 56.4 percent in 1976. At the same time, the percentage of blacks declined from 33.5 percent in 1972 to 29.0 percent the following year, followed by a series of fluctuations culminating in only a small percentage increase. Drug emergencies among Hispanics increased, however, from 4.9 percent in 1972 to 14.2 percent in 1974--a 190 percent increase--followed by a decline to 10.3 percent in 1976. These fluctuations may be a reflection of other changes within the Hispanic community. For one, the rapid increases in the Cuban and other Spanish-speaking populations in Dade County during recent years have been well documented, meaning that there was a larger base population for this ethnic cohort within which a drug emergency could occur. Secondly, while there was a tendency during the early 1970s for Hispanics to shy away from the services offered within the Anglo community, this phenomenon began to dissipate with more energetic outreach services in the Hispanic areas. And finally, the slight decline from 1974 to 1976 could be a reflection of the wider

TABLE 2.2

Basic Demographic Characteristics of 11,287 Drug-Emergency Patients, by Year

	1972		1973		1974		1975		1976	
	Number	Percent	Number	Percent	Number	Percent	Number	Percent	Number	Percent
Male	585	43.2	949	44.5	1,083	45.2	1,263	47.9	1,403	50.6
Female	769	56.8	1,179	55.4	1,314	54.8	1,373	52.0	1,365	49.3
No data	0	.0	1	.1	0	.0	1	.1	2	.1
17 and under	193	14.3	262	12.3	291	12.1	267	10.1	266	9.6
18-24	593	43.8	904	42.5	958	40.0	1,043	39.6	1,070	38.6
25-34	298	22.0	529	24.8	648	27.0	778	29.5	870	31.4
35-49	191	14.1	278	13.1	317	13.2	346	13.1	377	13.6
50 and over	68	5.0	130	6.1	158	6.6	168	6.4	163	5.9
No data	11	.8	26	1.2	25	1.1	35	1.3	24	.9
Black	454	33.5	616	29.0	746	31.1	891	33.8	909	32.8
Hispanic	66	4.9	226	10.6	341	14.2	313	11.9	285	10.3
White	832	61.5	1,282	60.2	1,301	54.3	1,419	53.8	1,562	56.4
No data	2	.1	5	.2	9	.4	14	.5	14	.5
Total	1,354	100.0	2,129	100.0	2,397	100.0	2,637	100.0	2,770	100.0

Source: Compiled by the authors.

11

structuring of emergency-room services in hospitals in the Hispanic areas of the county.

Table 2.2 also indicates that the age of the drug-emergency population is undergoing some transition. While 58.1 percent of the cases in 1972 were under age 25, this proportion declined to 48.2 percent by 1976. Concomitantly, while the 35-49-year and the 50-and-above age cohorts remained essentially unchanged, the percentage of drug emergencies within the 25-34-year age category increased by some 43 percent over the five-year period--from 22.0 percent in 1972 to 31.4 percent in 1976.

SUBSTANCE RESPONSIBLE FOR ADMISSION

An analysis of the drug emergencies by the primary substance involved shows that legally manufactured and distributed drugs have consistently accounted for a majority of the adverse reactions throughout the five-year period. However, a focused examination of these data by year and drug reflects some definite trends (see Table 2.3).

In 1972, some 41.4 percent of all acute/adverse reactions involved central-nervous-system depressants (barbiturates, other sedatives, and major and minor tranquilizers). As indicated below, this proportion has steadily declined since 1973:

Year	Percent of Reactions
1972	41.4
1973	42.2
1974	38.3
1975	36.9
1976	33.5

As indicated in Table 2.3, however, while reactions to tranquilizers have increased during this period, barbiturate and other sedative reactions sharply declined, likely the result of the tighter controls over barbiturates and methaqualone during recent years.

Central-nervous-system stimulants--antidepressants, amphetamines, and nonamphetamine stimulants (excluding cocaine)--accounted for relatively few problems in 1972 (3.9 percent), followed by a peak of 5.9 percent in 1973 and a decline to 4.4 percent in 1976.

Reactions to heroin reflect a fluctuating increase--12.6 percent in 1972, only 7.7 percent in 1973, and 14.0 percent in 1976. Even clearer patterns appear with respect to other illicit drugs. For example:

TABLE 2.3

Primary Substance Involved for 11,287 Drug-Emergency Patients, by Year

	1972		1973		1974		1975		1976	
	Number	Percent	Number	Percent	Number	Percent	Number	Percent	Number	Percent
Major tranquilizers	73	5.4	133	6.2	152	6.3	207	7.8	237	8.5
Minor tranquilizers	169	12.5	260	12.2	368	15.4	396	15.0	341	12.2
Barbiturates	175	13.0	284	13.3	229	9.6	197	7.5	194	7.0
Nonbarbiturate sedatives	131	9.7	206	9.7	161	6.7	163	6.2	155	5.6
Antidepressants	25	1.8	59	2.8	59	2.5	57	2.2	62	2.2
Amphetamines	11	.8	53	2.5	30	1.3	34	1.3	35	1.3
Nonamphetamine stimulants	17	1.3	12	.6	21	.9	28	1.1	24	.9
Narcotics	15	1.1	46	2.2	69	2.9	56	2.1	46	1.7
Methadone	33	2.4	72	3.4	65	2.7	94	3.6	68	2.5
Analgesics	42	3.1	68	3.2	107	4.5	80	3.0	85	3.1
Heroin	170	12.6	164	7.7	209	8.7	379	14.4	387	14.0
Cocaine	12	.9	25	1.2	34	1.4	47	1.8	69	2.5
Miscellaneous Rx.	49	3.6	100	4.7	139	5.8	165	6.3	210	7.6
Over-the-counter	102	7.5	148	7.0	178	7.4	149	5.6	142	5.1
Poisons	3	.2	8	.4	28	1.2	46	1.7	47	1.7
Hallucinogens	95	7.0	96	4.5	89	3.7	77	2.9	78	2.8
Marijuana	18	1.3	50	2.3	58	2.4	81	3.1	189	6.8
Inhalants	14	1.0	44	2.1	51	2.1	57	2.2	58	2.1
Unknown sedatives	11	.8	17	.8	8	.3	10	.4	6	.2
Unknown drugs	189	14.0	284	13.2	342	14.2	314	11.9	337	12.2
Total	1,354	100.0	2,129	100.0	2,397	100.0	2,637	100.0	2,770	100.0

Source: Compiled by the authors.

13

Drug	Year					Percent Change in Reactions
	1972	1973	1974	1975	1976	
Cocaine	.9%	1.2%	1.4%	1.8%	2.5%	+178
Hallucinogens	7.0	4.5	3.7	2.9	2.8	-60
Marijuana	1.3	2.3	2.4	3.1	6.8	+423

The widely suspected increasing usage in cocaine and marijuana and decreasing usage of hallucinogenic drugs receive some confirmation in these data. Reactions to cocaine proportionately increased by some 178 percent from 1972 through 1976; reactions to marijuana increased by some 423 percent, while reactions to the hallucinogenic drugs declined by 60 percent.

A proportional decline also appeared with respect to over-the-counter drugs, from 7.5 percent in 1972 to 5.1 percent in 1976, while reactions to solvents/inhalants more than doubled in proportional representation.

COMPLAINT AND CLINICAL STATUS
AT ADMISSION

Adverse drug reactions can encompass a wide variety of phenomena. For example:

- attempted suicide by drugs
- accidental overdose
- allergic reactions
- withdrawal and addiction problems
- infections
- psychotic and panic reactions
- extrapyramidal reaction (for example, muscle spasms)

In these data, accidental overdose represented by far the major drug reaction throughout the five-year period. Table 2.4, however, shows that overdose accounted for 62.3 percent of the cases in 1972, but had significantly declined to 43.6 percent by 1976. Similarly, there was a clear decline with respect to attempted suicide by drugs (17.2 percent to 6.4 percent). By contrast, there were significant increases with respect to allergic reactions, infections, psychotic/panic reactions, and extrapyramidal effects. The largest of these increases is that for psychotic and panic reactions, from 2.2 percent of the cases in 1972 to 18.2 percent in 1976, primarily related to the increased use of marijuana in the Dade County population during the study period.

TABLE 2.4

Complaint at Admission of 11,287 Drug-Emergency Patients, by Year

	1972		1973		1974		1975		1976	
	Number	Percent	Number	Percent	Number	Percent	Number	Percent	Number	Percent
Attempted suicide	233	17.2	476	22.4	557	23.2	408	15.5	178	6.4
Overdose	843	62.3	1,100	51.7	1,113	46.4	1,111	42.1	1,206	43.6
Allergic reaction	5	.4	45	2.1	92	3.8	127	4.8	117	4.2
Withdrawal	80	5.9	176	8.3	152	6.3	219	8.3	181	6.5
Physical addiction	28	2.1	54	2.5	124	5.2	144	5.5	149	5.4
Infections, localized	3	.2	4	.2	12	.5	24	.9	17	.6
Infections, systemic	25	1.8	43	2.0	44	1.9	60	2.3	102	3.7
Psychotic/panic reactions	30	2.2	184	8.6	254	10.6	322	12.2	503	18.2
Public intoxication	5	.4	1	.1	0	.0	26	.9	20	.7
Extrapyramidal effects	0	.0	7	.3	10	.4	86	3.3	134	4.8
ETOH* seizures	0	.0	0	.0	0	.0	4	.2	6	.2
Delirium tremens	0	.0	0	.0	0	.0	0	.0	3	.1
Cirrhosis, GI problems	0	.0	0	.0	1	.1	12	.5	27	1.0
Other	2	.1	18	.8	6	.3	64	2.4	125	4.5
Unknown	100	7.4	21	1.0	32	1.3	30	1.1	2	.1
Total	1,354	100.0	2,129	100.0	2,397	100.0	2,637	100.0	2,770	100.0

*Alcohol.

Source: Compiled by the authors.

15

A patient's clinical status at the time of admission to the emergency room was not recorded during the early years of this project, but was available for the period 1974 through 1976. As indicated in Table 2.5, the vast majority of patients are conscious at the time of admission, and this increased from 83.9 percent in 1974 to 92.2 percent in 1976.

DISPOSITION

Dispositional data were collected for all drug-emergency patients beginning in 1973. As indicated in Table 2.6, the majority of cases were either treated and released, or treated and released with a referral to some other community agency for followup care. Few patients left before treatment was administered or left against medical advice, and a small segment were treated and admitted to medical or psychiatric wards for further care. An additional cohort (12.4 percent in 1976) were in police custody at the time of admission and were jailed subsequent to treatment.

The overwhelming majority of drug-emergency patients were not referred to some other service agency (74 percent in 1976). As suggested by Table 2.7, most of those who were referred were offered the hospital's crisis intervention clinic, or the Dade County Comprehensive Drug Program. The clinic was utilized primarily for panic-reaction and attempted-suicide cases, while the Comprehensive Drug Program referrals were primarily heroin users. (This program and the subject of agency referrals are discussed in detail in Chapters 5 and 6.)

DRUG CATEGORY TRENDS

It can be seen in the preceding data that the acute-drug-reactions population has been undergoing some change, and that the nature of the drugs involved has also undergone change. Of importance, as well, are the alterations in the characteristics of those persons associated with the major drug categories. In this section, the focus is placed on the static and dynamic characteristics of the drug-emergency patients appearing for adverse effects to the five major legal and three major illegal substances. The changing sex ratios on a year-to-year basis appear in Table 2.8. It can be readily seen that acute reactions to major tranquilizers became increasingly common among males. That is, during 1972, only 35.6 percent of the patients with acute reactions to major tranquilizers were males, but by 1976, males represented 54.4 percent of these cases. Similarly, male

TABLE 2.5

Clinical Status at Admission of 7,804 Drug–Emergency Patients, 1974–76, by Year

	1974		1975		1976	
	Number	Percent	Number	Percent	Number	Percent
Conscious and coherent	1,551	64.7	1,937	73.4	2,012	72.6
Conscious and incoherent	460	19.2	424	16.1	542	19.6
Unconscious	320	13.4	200	7.6	139	5.0
Dead	3	.1	3	.1	--	--
No data	63	2.6	73	2.8	77	2.8
Total	2,397	100.0	2,637	100.0	2,770	100.0

Source: Compiled by the authors.

TABLE 2.6

Disposition of 9,933 Drug–Emergency Patients, 1973–76, by Year

	1973		1974		1975		1976	
	Number	Percent	Number	Percent	Number	Percent	Number	Percent
Left without treatment	74	3.5	116	4.8	99	3.8	92	3.3
Treated and released	950	44.6	725	30.2	804	30.5	889	32.1
Treated, left against medical advice	107	5.0	153	6.4	119	4.5	134	4.8
Treated and referred	295	13.9	621	25.9	710	26.9	717	25.9
Treated, admitted to psychiatry	115	5.4	239	10.0	216	8.2	311	11.2
Treated, admitted to medical ward	159	7.5	169	7.1	298	11.3	262	9.5
Treated and jailed	399	18.7	292	12.2	351	13.3	344	12.4
No data	30	1.4	82	3.4	40	1.5	21	.8
Total	2,129	100.0	2,397	100.0	2,637	100.0	2,770	100.0

Source: Compiled by the authors.

TABLE 2.7

Community Service Agency Referrals among 9,933 Drug Emergency Patients, by Year

	1973		1974		1975		1976	
	Number	Percent	Number	Percent	Number	Percent	Number	Percent
Comprehensive alcohol program	0	.0	16	.6	17	.6	92	3.2
Comprehensive drug program	88	4.1	166	6.9	151	5.7	139	5.0
Crisis intervention clinic	105	4.9	213	8.9	305	11.6	307	11.1
Outpatient department	3	.1	2	.1	9	.3	10	.4
Other hospital	23	1.1	53	2.2	47	1.8	49	1.8
Private psychiatrist	10	.5	50	2.1	28	1.1	24	.9
Jackson Memorial Hospital detoxification unit	4	.2	19	.8	10	.4	1	.1
Welfare	29	1.4	55	2.3	52	2.0	36	1.3
Other social service agency	33	1.6	50	2.1	77	2.9	62	2.2
Not referred	1,834	86.1	1,773	74.0	1,927	73.1	2,050	74.0
Unknown	0	.0	0	.0	14	.5	0	.0
Total	2,129	100.0	2,397	100.0	2,637	100.0	2,770	100.0

Source: Compiled by the authors.

TABLE 2.8

Sex Distribution, in Percentages, for Patients with Adverse Reactions to Selected Drug Types, by Year

	1972 (N = 933)		1973 (N = 1,341)		1974 (N = 1,444)		1975 (N = 1,649)		1976 (N = 1,723)	
	Male	Female	Male	Female	Male	Female	Male	Female	Male	Female
Major tranquilizers	35.6	64.4	36.8	63.2	40.1	59.9	44.9	55.1	54.4	45.6
Minor tranquilizers	24.9	75.1	27.3	72.7	25.0	75.0	33.3	66.7	33.4	66.6
Barbiturates	39.4	60.6	48.2	51.8	48.9	51.1	47.7	52.3	50.0	50.0
Nonbarbiturate sedatives	43.5	56.5	53.4	46.6	37.9	62.1	49.1	50.9	58.7	41.2
Heroin	52.9	47.1	53.7	46.3	56.0	44.0	58.6	41.4	53.2	46.8
Over-the-counter substances	26.5	73.5	22.3	77.7	28.7	71.3	29.5	70.5	44.4	55.6
Hallucinogens	72.6	27.4	76.0	24.0	71.9	28.1	77.9	22.1	82.1	17.9
Marijuana	88.9	11.1	78.0	22.0	70.7	29.3	72.8	27.2	65.1	34.9
Central-nervous-system depressants (all types)	35.4	64.6	41.6	58.4	35.8	64.2	41.4	58.6	46.5	53.5

Source: Compiled by the authors.

19

TABLE 2.9

Racial/Ethnic Distribution, in Percentages, for Patients with Adverse Reactions to Selected Drug Types, by Year

	1972 (N = 933)			1973 (N = 1,341)			1974 (N = 1,444)			1975 (N = 1,649)			1976 (N = 1,723)		
	Black	Hispanic	White	Black	Hispanic	White	Black	Hispanic	White	Black	Hispanic	White	Black	Hispanic	White
Major tranquilizers	20.5	5.5	74.0	29.3	13.5	57.1	26.3	12.5	61.2	31.4	17.9	50.7	27.0	16.0	56.9
Minor tranquilizers	26.6	8.3	65.1	18.5	21.9	59.6	23.4	24.7	51.9	18.4	22.5	59.1	14.7	18.8	66.6
Barbiturates	27.4	5.1	67.4	14.8	7.0	78.2	13.5	7.9	78.6	16.8	7.6	75.6	8.8	5.2	86.1
Nonbarbiturate sedatives	13.7	3.1	83.2	13.1	9.7	77.2	11.2	14.9	73.9	7.4	12.9	79.7	11.6	9.0	79.4
All central-nervous-system depressants	23.0	5.7	71.4	13.0	69.3	19.2	19.2	16.7	64.1	19.0	16.8	64.2	16.1	13.6	70.3
Heroin	59.4	2.4	38.2	67.7	3.0	29.3	58.9	7.7	33.5	64.4	3.7	31.9	61.5	5.4	33.1
Over-the-counter substances	49.0	8.8	42.2	50.7	11.5	37.8	46.7	18.0	35.4	46.3	13.4	40.3	47.2	10.6	42.3
Hallucinogens	24.2	3.2	72.6	13.5	9.4	77.0	18.0	5.6	76.4	13.0	9.1	77.9	7.7	9.0	83.3
Marijuana	33.3	5.6	61.1	22.0	14.0	64.0	37.9	15.5	46.6	22.2	7.4	70.3	25.9	6.3	67.7

Source: Compiled by the authors.

involvement also increased with respect to the minor tranquilizers, barbiturates, nonbarbiturate sedatives, over-the-counter drugs, and hallucinogens. However, also of interest in these data are the increasing percentages of marijuana reactions among women (from 11.1 percent in 1972 to 34.9 percent by 1976), and the consistently high percentages of women within the heroin category.

In Table 2.9, it can be seen that among blacks, there have been notable increases only with respect to major tranquilizers, with major decreases in most other areas. The percentage of Hispanics increased during the early 1970s, followed by decreases by the end of the study period, in most categories, while whites demonstrated significant increases only with respect to barbiturates, hallucinogens, and marijuana.

Table 2.10 provides data on median age. Interestingly, within the category of central-nervous-system depressants, in the 1972-76 period the median age of the major- and minor-tranquilizer patients decreased, while the age in the sedative categories increased. The increase in median age for heroin cases is striking (from 21.5 to 24), and increases also appeared with respect to patients being treated for acute reactions to over-the-counter drugs, hallucinogens, and marijuana.

TABLE 2.10

Median Age of Patients with Adverse Reactions
to Selected Drug Types, by Year

	1972	1973	1974	1975	1976
Central-nervous-system depressants (all)	24.0	24.6	25.0	25.5	25.5
Major tranquilizers	27.1	27.9	25.4	25.7	25.9
Minor tranquilizers	28.6	29.5	28.4	29.1	27.7
Barbiturates	22.5	23.2	22.9	23.7	24.2
Nonbarbiturate sedatives	22.4	22.3	23.2	22.3	23.1
Heroin	21.5	21.8	22.6	24.0	24.0
Over-the-counter substances	22.7	21.6	23.2	22.4	23.9
Hallucinogens	18.8	20.6	20.4	21.5	21.4
Marijuana	20.5	21.9	20.5	21.4	21.8

Source: Compiled by the authors.

TABLE 2.11

Complaint at Admission, in Percentages, of Patients with Adverse Reactions to Selected Drug Types, by Year

	Attempted Suicide	Overdose	Addiction Related	Psychotic/panic Reaction	Other
1972					
Central-nervous-system depressants	26.8	60.7	4.2	.7	7.5
Major tranquilizers	26.0	64.4	1.4	1.4	(6.8)
Minor tranquilizers	33.7	58.0	2.4	.0	5.9
Barbiturates	22.9	63.4	5.8	.6	7.4
Nonbarbiturate sedatives	23.7	58.8	6.1	1.6	9.9
Heroin	1.2	48.8	45.9	.6	3.5
Over-the-counter substances	35.3	62.7	.0	.0	2.0
Hallucinogens	2.1	55.8	1.1	16.9	24.2
Marijuana	.0	72.2	11.2	11.2	5.5
1973					
Central-nervous-system depressants	31.5	55.2	7.1	3.6	2.6
Major tranquilizers	38.3	48.1	.8	4.6	8.3
Minor tranquilizers	49.2	43.1	3.5	2.3	2.0
Barbiturates	23.6	61.3	12.0	1.4	1.8
Nonbarbiturate sedatives	15.5	66.5	9.3	7.8	1.0
Heroin	1.2	23.2	66.5	4.9	4.2
Over-the-counter substances	48.0	49.3	.7	1.4	.7
Hallucinogens	1.0	41.7	1.0	56.2	.0
Marijuana	.0	36.0	42.0	22.0	.0

1974

Central-nervous-system depressants	31.6	54.4	6.2	3.7	4.1
Major tranquilizers	28.3	50.0	.7	3.9	17.1
Minor tranquilizers	45.7	49.7	.3	2.7	1.6
Barbiturates	15.3	60.3	17.9	4.4	2.1
Nonbarbiturate sedatives	26.1	60.9	8.0	4.9	.0
Heroin	2.4	30.1	60.3	4.8	2.4
Over-the-counter substances	44.9	48.9	.0	.0	6.3
Hallucinogens	1.1	13.5	1.1	80.9	3.3
Marijuana	1.7	15.5	8.6	70.7	3.4

1975

Central-nervous-system depressants	21.9	52.6	6.9	5.4	13.2
Major tranquilizers	17.9	35.3	.5	1.5	45.0
Minor tranquilizers	30.3	57.3	4.0	4.3	4.0
Barbiturates	16.8	47.2	20.3	9.1	6.5
Nonbarbiturate sedatives	12.9	69.9	5.5	8.5	3.0
Heroin	1.3	32.2	52.0	2.4	9.0
Over-the-counter substances	35.6	49.0	.7	1.4	13.5
Hallucinogens	.0	16.9	7.8	72.7	2.6
Marijuana	2.5	22.2	3.7	60.5	11.2

1976

Central-nervous-system depressants	9.9	56.6	6.3	9.9	17.3
Major tranquilizers	6.3	30.0	.4	4.6	58.7
Minor tranquilizers	14.7	70.1	2.6	9.4	3.3
Barbiturates	7.7	59.3	15.4	13.9	3.5
Nonbarbiturate sedatives	7.7	64.5	11.6	14.2	1.9
Heroin	.8	17.8	56.4	14.7	9.6
Over-the-counter substances	16.2	63.4	.0	2.8	17.5
Hallucinogens	.0	25.6	.0	68.0	6.4
Marijuana	.0	19.6	4.2	70.3	5.9

Source: Compiled by the authors.

As suggested by Table 2.11, changes also took place with respect to drug categories and complaint at admission. For example:

□ The involvement of central-nervous-system depressants in attempted suicides and in accidental overdoses has clearly declined, with allergic and panic/psychotic reactions to these drugs increasing.

□ The role of heroin has declined with respect to suicide attempts and overdose, but has increased regarding the incidence of addiction problems and psychotic reactions presented at the emergency room.

□ The proportional incidence of accidental overdose related to over-the-counter drugs was essentially the same at the beginning and the end of the study period, but there was a clear decline in their relation to attempted suicide.

□ With respect to hallucinogenic drugs, their involvement in overdose declined, while they were totally ceasing as a mechanism of attempted suicide; conversely, psychotic/panic reactions increased.

□ Marijuana overdose cases have proportionately declined, but with respect to psychotic/panic reactions, the percent change over the five-year period has been +528 percent.

ALCOHOL EMERGENCIES

The one major drug category which has not yet been discussed in this study is alcohol. Beginning in July of 1975, the Acute Drug Reactions Project started collection of baseline data on acute alcohol reactions at the Jackson Memorial Hospital emergency room, gathering the same kind of information obtained for all the (other) drug-emergency cases. For the period from July 1, 1975 through December 31, 1976, a total of 5,004 alcohol-emergency patients were seen (compared to 4,054 drug-emergency patients for the same period). Because these two populations tended to differ in socially significant ways, however, information on them was analyzed separately. The data on the alcohol-emergency patients are reported in Chapter 6, along with their specific differences from the other adverse-reaction patients.

SUMMARY

In summary, these initial baseline data suggest that the hospital emergency room occupies a conspicuous position in the drug treatment service-delivery network. The data in this section have reflected on some 11,287 drug cases over a five-year period, indicating, with 5,004 alcohol patients recorded during an 18-month period, that the Jackson Memorial Hospital emergency room currently has contact with almost 6,500 persons with a substance-related problem annually. This suggests that the hospital emergency room can play a significant role as a data collection base for studying substance-abuse trends, and as a mechanism for treatment intervention and referral.

The drug data reported here have readily demonstrated that, at least within this population base, the nature of substance abuse may be changing, and characteristics of drug users may also be undergoing some alteration. In later chapters of this book, these points are further examined in terms of their significance and their utility for treatment and policy planning.

3

PUBLIC VERSUS PRIVATE HOSPITALS: DRUG-EMERGENCY PATIENTS AT JACKSON MEMORIAL HOSPITAL VERSUS OTHER DADE COUNTY HOSPITALS

Data from the first three years of the Acute Drug Reactions Project indicated that individuals with Spanish surnames were underrepresented in the emergency-room facilities at Jackson Memorial Hospital. In order to investigate this phenomenon, the ADRP contacted the directors of several private hospitals with emergency-room facilities located in primarily Hispanic neighborhoods. The purpose was to determine if these hospitals were receiving Hispanic drug-emergency patients. Given the willingness of these hospitals to participate, all remaining hospitals in Dade County having emergency-treatment facilities were contacted in order to obtain a better indication of drug-related emergencies throughout the county.

There are 24 hospitals in Dade County with emergency-room facilities, other than Jackson Memorial Hospital. Of these 24, 12 were eager to participate in the research endeavor, seven indicated that they only had two or three drug-related cases per year (several of these hospitals participated in the collection of DAWN data and their statements were verified), and five hospitals refused to participate. Of the five refusals, three were small hospitals whose rates of drug-related cases were expected to be low, and two were large hospitals. These institutions stated that their participation would violate patient confidentiality and that involvement with outside research projects in the past had resulted in legal ramifications.

Within the 12 participating hospitals, emergency-room records for the calendar year 1975 were assessed. Since these hospitals did not maintain a separate file for drug cases, every emergency-room record had to be examined to determine its relevance for the study. When a patient record was designated by project staff as involving an acute drug reaction, the appropriate information was transferred to the data collection form used at Jackson Memorial Hospital to insure comparability of data (see Form A in the Appendix).

FINDINGS

   As shown in Table 3.1, drug-emergency patients in Dade
County's other hospitals were considerably different from those at
Jackson Memorial Hospital. Almost two-thirds (65.1 percent) were
females as opposed to 51.1 percent at Jackson Memorial Hospital.
The other hospitals also reflected a higher proportion of Hispanics
as compared to Jackson Memorial (15.8 percent versus 11.9 percent) and a lower proportion of blacks (3.3 percent versus 33.8
percent). In terms of age, the Jackson patients were clustered in
the adolescent and young adult cohorts with 79.2 percent under age
35, while the patients in the other hospitals were more widely distributed over the age spectrum.

TABLE 3.1

Basic Demographic Characteristics of Drug-Emergency
Patients: Jackson Memorial Hospital versus Other
Dade County Hospitals

	Other Hospitals		Jackson Memorial Hospital	
	Number	Percent	Number	Percent
Male	491	33.4	1,263	47.9
Female	957	65.1	1,373	52.1
Unknown	22	1.5	1	—
Black	49	3.3	891	33.8
Hispanic	232	15.8	313	11.9
White	822	55.9	1,419	53.8
Unknown	367	25.0	14	.5
17 and under	313	21.3	267	10.1
18-24	370	25.2	1,043	39.6
25-34	323	22.0	778	29.5
35-49	263	17.9	346	13.1
50 and above	196	13.3	168	6.4
Unknown	5	.3	35	1.3
Total	1,470	100.0	2,637	100.0

Source: Compiled by the authors.

The data suggest that the other hospitals in Dade County dealt only minimally with acute or adverse reactions to illicit substances. Table 3.2 confirms this, since 45.4 percent of the other hospitals' drug emergencies involved central-nervous-system depressants, and at least 75.7 percent of the cases involved legally manufactured and distributed drugs. It would seem that only a minimal proportion of reactions to illicit substances were treated at these hospitals, especially those involving the most notorious of the illicit substances. Specifically, although Jackson Memorial had a total of less than twice as many drug-emergency patients as the other hospitals, it had over three times as many marijuana and hallucinogen cases, almost five times as many inhalant cases, and over nine times as many heroin and cocaine cases. In discussing this pattern with physicians, hospital staff, emergency-room attendants, ambulance personnel, and patients, it became clear that most of the other hospitals in Dade County were unwilling to treat cases which they judged to be "street drug abusers." In fact, it was learned that when heroin overdose cases were presented at these hospitals, in the majority of cases the patient would be rerouted to Jackson Memorial Hospital for treatment. In addition, because these other hospitals were private institutions, in the majority of cases they took only those patients with a demonstrated ability to pay for their emergency-room costs, while transferring other patients to Jackson.

A related phenomenon is reflected in Table 3.3, which shows that accidental overdose was the complaint at admission for most of the other hospitals' drug-emergency patients—72.5 percent as opposed to 42.1 percent at Jackson Memorial Hospital. By contrast, these hospitals dealt with only a minimal percentage of withdrawal or addiction problems (1.7 percent), psychotic/panic reactions (0.7 percent), or alcohol-related problems (0.3 percent). Again, this is likely a manifestation of the drug-using types accepted for treatment at these private hospitals.

The vast majority of patients in all hospitals were conscious at their time of admission, making the figures for the other hospitals highly similar to those reported in Table 2.5 for Jackson Memorial.

The difference between the populations treated by Jackson Memorial Hospital and those treated by the other hospitals is again reflected, however, in the disposition of patients. As indicated in Table 3.4, drug-emergency patients in the other hospitals were either treated and released, referred, or admitted to a hospital medical unit. In contrast with Jackson Memorial Hospital, few were transferred to a psychiatric unit or jailed after treatment. About the same percentage of patients were referred by these other hospitals, but their referrals are much likelier than Jackson Memorial's to be to private psychiatrists (see Table 3.5). In fact, over

TABLE 3.2

Primary Substance Involved for Drug-Emergency
Patients: Jackson Memorial Hospital versus
Other Dade County Hospitals

	Other Hospitals		Jackson Memorial Hospital	
	Number	Percent	Number	Percent
Major tranquilizers	94	6.4	207	7.8
Minor tranquilizers	365	24.8	396	15.0
Barbiturates	108	7.3	197	7.5
Nonbarbiturate sedatives	98	6.7	163	6.2
Antidepressants	51	3.5	57	2.2
Amphetamines	14	1.0	34	1.3
Nonamphetamine stimulants	9	.6	28	1.1
Narcotics	50	3.4	56	2.1
Analgesics	60	4.1	80	3.0
Heroin	38	2.6	379	14.4
Cocaine	5	.3	47	1.8
Miscellaneous prescriptions	149	10.1	165	6.3
Over-the- counter	184	12.5	149	5.7
Poisons	73	5.0	46	1.7
Hallucinogens	23	1.6	77	2.9
Marijuana	24	1.6	81	3.1
Inhalants	12	.8	57	2.2
Unknown sedatives	3	.2	10	.4
Methadone	—	—	94	3.6
Unknown drugs	110	7.5	313	11.9
Total	1,470	100.0	2,637	100.0

Source: Compiled by the authors.

29

TABLE 3.3

Complaint at Admission of Drug-Emergency Patients: Jackson Memorial Hospital versus Other Dade County Hospitals

	Other Hospitals		Jackson Memorial Hospital	
	Number	Percent	Number	Percent
Attempted suicide	116	8.0	408	15.5
Accidental overdose	1,066	72.5	1,111	42.1
Allergic reaction	188	12.8	127	4.8
Withdrawal	14	1.0	219	8.3
Physical addiction	11	.7	144	5.5
Infections, localized	—	—	24	.9
Infections, systemic	2	.1	60	2.3
Psychotic or panic reactions	11	.7	322	12.2
Public intoxication	1	.1	26	.9
Extrapyramidal effects	4	.3	86	3.3
ETOH* seizures	—	—	4	.2
Delirium tremens	—	—	0	.0
Cirrhosis, G.I. problems	3	.2	12	.5
Other	49	3.3	64	2.4
Unknown	5	.3	30	1.1
Total	1,470	100.0	2,637	100.0

*Alcohol.
Source: Compiled by the authors.

TABLE 3.4

Disposition of Drug-Emergency Patients: Jackson Memorial
Hospital versus Other Dade County Hospitals

	Other Hospitals		Jackson Memorial Hospital	
	Number	Percent	Number	Percent
Left without treatment	20	1.4	99	3.8
Treated and released	732	49.8	804	30.5
Treated, left against medical advice	54	3.7	119	4.5
Treated and referred	369	25.1	710	26.9
Treated, admitted to psychiatry	1	<.1	216	8.2
Treated, admitted to medical unit	280	19.0	298	11.3
Treated and jailed	2	.1	351	13.3
Dead	7	.5	6	.2
Unknown	5	.3	34	1.3
Total	1,470	100.0	2,637	100.0

Source: Compiled by the authors.

TABLE 3.5

Community Service Agency Referrals for Drug-Emergency Patients:
Jackson Memorial Hospital versus Other Dade County Hospitals

	Other Hospitals		Jackson Memorial Hospital	
	Number	Percent	Number	Percent
Comprehensive alcohol program	—	—	17	.6
Comprehensive drug program	7	.5	151	5.7
Crisis intervention clinic	98	6.7	305	11.6
Outpatient department	1	<.1	9	.3
Other hospital	47	3.2	47	1.8
Private psychiatrist	204	13.9	28	1.1
Jackson Memorial detoxification unit	2	<.1	10	.4
Welfare	2	.1	52	2.0
Other social service agencies	8	.5	77	2.9
No referral	1,101	74.9	1,927	73.1
Unknown	—	—	14	.5
Total	1,470	100.0	2,637	100.0

Source: Compiled by the authors.

half the other hospitals' referrals were to private psychiatrists, compared to only 4 percent of Jackson Memorial's referrals. The other hospitals also referred patients to another hospital much more often than did Jackson Memorial (12.7 percent versus 6.6 percent of the referrals—or 39.3 percent versus 6.6 percent when referrals to Jackson Memorial's crisis intervention clinic are counted). By contrast, 43 percent of the Jackson patients were treated at the hospital's own crisis center; this was followed by a heavy reliance on substance-abuse programs (23.7 percent), community agencies (10.8 percent), and public assistance (7.3 percent)—three kinds of agencies accounting for fewer than 5 percent of the other hospitals' referrals.

INTERPRETATION

These data clearly suggest that Jackson Memorial Hospital and the other hospitals in Dade County service different drug-emergency populations. As noted earlier, this is partially due to the other hospitals' unwillingness to accept "drug abusers" or persons of minimal financial stability. But other sources of population differences also exist.

The age differences can be partially explained by structural differences in the emergency rooms. The emergency facilities at Jackson Memorial Hospital are divided into several separate units, one of which is pediatrics. However, emergency rooms at the other hospitals treat all age groups together and combine their medical records. This tends to inflate the proportion of cases under 18 in the other hospitals. The age differences seen at the upper end of the age continuum, on the other hand, are related to the type of drug used. Prescription-drug-related reactions are more prevalent among older people than are illicit-drug-related incidents. Since the other hospitals accept fewer illicit-drug users, it would be expected that their population would also have more older patients as well as having more young ones. Conversely, since the 18-24 and 25-34 age cohorts are more likely to include the illicit-drug users and since Jackson Memorial Hospital was more likely than the other hospitals to treat their drug reactions, it is expected that their population would cluster in these age categories, rather than being more equally distributed as at the other hospitals.

The unwillingness or inability of the other hospitals to collect racial or ethnic data made it difficult to fully address such distributions. In fact, ethnicity was unknown for 25 percent of the other hospitals' patients. By examining Spanish surnames in these other hospitals' files, significant numbers of Hispanics were discovered.

The medical staff at private hospitals tended to be somewhat more cautious than the medical staff at Jackson Memorial Hospital in diagnosing the medical reason for a patient's seeking treatment. This cautious diagnostic approach to some extent explained the smaller percentage of attempted-suicide cases treated at the other hospitals. Often, a patient's private physician would be contacted by the emergency-room staff at these other hospitals. It was learned that these private physicians were less willing to include "suicide attempt" in their patient's file unless it was clearly indicated.

Perhaps of greatest importance in these data is the further documentation of a prescription-drug problem in Dade County. A high incidence of prescription-drug abuse and accidental overdose through self-medication was evident in the Jackson Memorial Hospital emergency-room population. However, it appeared to be even more evident in the other Dade County hospital populations. At these private hospitals, four out of every five drug-emergency cases included licit drugs: tranquilizers, sedatives, analgesics, antidepressants, other prescription drugs, and over-the-counter preparations. The users of these drugs represent a population that have become dysfunctional, or are at high risk of becoming dysfunctional, as a result of this abuse or self-medication, in a setting where available drug treatment services have not been geared for their management.

4

DETAILED INTERVIEW DATA: A COMPARISON OF DRUG-EMERGENCY PATIENTS IN MIAMI AND DENVER

With the onset of the fourth year of the Acute Drug Reactions Project, when attempts were made to develop a nationwide consortium, an extensive interview instrument was structured for collecting standardized data on a subpopulation of patients in each of the cities. Although the consortium never materialized (see Chapter 1), the instrument was implemented in Denver in July 1975 and in Miami during August 1975. The purpose of the extended interview (Form B in the Appendix) was to understand more about the drug-emergency patient--social and personal characteristics, drug use and treatment history, arrest history, and other salient phenomena in the individual's life which might serve to improve the understanding of this population of drug users.

Not all drug-emergency patients were interviewed during this phase of the project. A total of 4,054 acute-drug-reactions patients were seen at Miami's Jackson Memorial Hospital between July 1, 1975 and December 31, 1976, and of these, only 309 received an extensive interview. In Denver, 527 drug-emergency patients were interviewed; this is a larger number of interviews than were done in Miami, but still only a fraction of all drug-emergency patients seen at Denver General Hospital. This selecting-out process was not dictated by any scientific sampling techniques, but rather, it was the result of such limitations on the availability of patients as the following:

- □ Not all patients were willing to be interviewed.
- □ Not all patients were coherent at the time of interviewer contact.
- □ Numerous patients left the hospital premises prior to a medical discharge and before they could be contacted by an interviewer.
- □ Many patients were admitted to the medical or psychiatric units of the hospital and were unavailable for an interview.
- □ Several patients were placed in custody and could not be interviewed.

□ Some patients were Spanish-speaking and bilingual interviewers were not always available.

The result of these problems was a bias in the interviewing procedures toward more serious cases. That is, the more life-threatening the drug and the more serious the adverse reaction to it, the longer the patient was likely to remain in the emergency room to receive the full examination and treatment; the longer the patient was there, in turn, the higher the chances of the interviewer being able to talk to him or her. On the other hand, the most extremely serious cases--in which the patient was unconscious and/or rushed immediately into treatment and then to an intensive care ward--were also excluded from the sample. Nonetheless, the discrepancies between the populations and the samples are perhaps fewer than one might expect, given the necessarily nonrandom sampling procedures employed (see Table 4.1). Differences in sex and age composition are minor, except that the interview sample contained only about a third as many persons under age 18 as one would expect from their representation in the population of all drug-emergency patients (9.6 percent). Blacks are also underrepresented in the interview sample, but to a relatively minor degree (32.4 percent of the population; 26.5 percent of the sample).

There was also a difference between the population and sample in the matter of which substances were involved in adverse drug reactions: heroin and the central-nervous-system (CNS) depressants (sedatives and tranquilizers) are overrepresented in the sample while marijuana, hallucinogens, and inhalants are underrepresented. Even here, however, most of the differences are small (with the notable exception of the sedatives, which are involved for only about 13 percent of the population, but 26 percent of the sample), and it might also be noted that about 5 percent more of the interview sample than of the population cases could be identified as to substance involved. As with the demographic differences, these population-sample discrepancies also seem to point to a bias toward the more serious drug emergencies in the interviewing procedures. However, the clear overrepresentation of sedative cases does at least provide a likely explanation for the racial difference previously noted. That is, while a large proportion of drug-reaction cases interviewed involved CNS depressants, Dade County blacks generally have a lower incidence of CNS-depressant reactions than would be expected from their numbers in the general population (in Dade County, 15 percent; versus, for example, among sedative and tranquilizer deaths, according to 1971-75 Dade County Medical Examiner records, under 2 percent).

To summarize these data, the interview sample is not totally representative of the drug-emergency population from which it was drawn. However, the methodological bias toward inclusion of the more serious cases does enable us to examine detailed social background factors for some of those patients most obviously in need of social services of some type. Further, as discussed above, the differences between the sample and population distributions on sex, race and ethnicity, and age are of relatively insignificant size; and most of the differences in drug type--except for the overrepresentation of sedatives--are even smaller. In short, even though random sampling procedures could not be used, the interviewed patients seem sufficiently representative of all drug-emergency patients to make the detailed interview data helpful in understanding the drug-emergency phenomenon.

Patient interviews were anonymous. All subjects were told the nature of the research and asked to sign an informed-consent release. In all, 309 drug cases were interviewed in Miami and 527 drug cases were interviewed in Denver. In the analysis that follows, these samples are described and contrasted. In addition, the data on narcotics users, sedative users, and minor-tranquilizer users are examined separately and compared to each other in the final section of this chapter.

SOCIAL AND DEMOGRAPHIC CHARACTERISTICS

As indicated in Table 4.1, the two emergency-room samples were somewhat different in sex and ethnic composition. While 52.4 percent of the Miami patients interviewed were males, only 44.2 percent of the Denver patients were. Whites comprised over 60 percent of both samples, but blacks were more numerous in the Miami than in the Denver sample (26.5 percent versus 12.0 percent), and the reverse was true for Hispanics (9.4 percent in Miami, 24.7 percent in Denver). The age distributions for the two cities were roughly the same, with only a slightly greater proportion of older patients in the Denver sample. The respective median ages for the Miami and Denver patients were 26 and 27 years.

Considering that only 16.6 percent of the interviewed patients were under 21, a rather large proportion (40.2 percent) were persons who had never married. In addition, as Table 4.2 indicates, of the 500 patients who had been married, 279 (55.8 percent) were separated or divorced by the time of the interview. The two city samples were fairly similar in this regard, with the slightly higher rate of never-married patients in Miami being predictable from its slightly younger age distribution. Table 4.2 also shows, however, that only a minority (26.1 percent) of the patients were living alone, with differences between the two samples in living arrangements again being small and what one might expect from the slightly different age distributions.

TABLE 4.1

Basic Demographic Characteristics of Drug-Emergency Patients Interviewed in Two Cities, and of All Jackson Memorial Hospital Drug-Emergency Patients Seen, July 1975 through December 1976

	Miami		Denver		JMH* (N = 4,054)
	Number	Percent	Number	Percent	Percent
Males	162	52.4	233	44.2	49.8
Females	147	47.6	294	55.8	50.2
White	193	62.5	317	60.2	57.0
Black	82	26.5	63	12.0	32.4
Hispanic	29	9.4	130	24.7	10.1
Native American	2	.6	11	2.1 ⎫	
Other	2	.6	6	1.1 ⎬	.6
No data	1	.3	--	-- ⎭	
17 years or less	10	3.2	20	3.8	9.6
18-24 years	118	38.2	176	33.4	38.4
25-34 years	117	37.9	202	38.3	31.1
35-49 years	42	13.6	86	16.3	13.6
50 years and above	22	7.1	41	7.8	6.2
No data	--	--	2	6.4	1.1
Total	309	100.0	527	100.0	100.0

*Jackson Memorial Hospital. Data on drug-emergency patients at JMH are included for comparison with the Miami (JMH) interview sample; see the discussion in the first section of this chapter.

Source: Compiled by the authors.

Table 4.3 shows that the two samples were also very similar in terms of educational attainment. About 45 percent of both sets of patients had less than a high-school education and only about 12 percent had a higher certification than a high-school diploma (about half of which was attributable to vocational certifications, as opposed

TABLE 4.2

Marital Status and Living Arrangements of Drug-Emergency
Patients Interviewed in Two Cities

	Miami		Denver		Total	
	Number	Percent	Number	Percent	Number	Percent
Never married	134	43.4	202	38.3	336	40.2
Married[a]	67	21.7	135	25.6	192	23.0
Separated, divorced	103	33.3	176	33.4	279	33.4
Widowed	5	1.6	14	2.7	19	2.3
Living alone	70	22.7	148	28.1	218	26.1
Living with:						
spouse	52	16.8	117	22.2	169	20.2
parents	61	19.7	66	12.5	127	15.2
other relatives[b]	46	14.9	82	15.6	128	15.3
friend/other	73	23.6	105	19.9	178	21.3
institution	7	2.3	9	1.7	16	1.9
No data	--	--	1	.2	1	.1
Total	309	100.0	527	100.0	836	100.0

[a]Including common law.
[b]Including children.
Source: Compiled by the authors.

TABLE 4.3

Educational Attainment of Drug-Emergency Patients
Interviewed in Two Cities

	Miami		Denver		Total	
	Number	Percent	Number	Percent	Number	Percent
0-7 years	17	5.5	33	6.3	50	6.0
8-11 years	118	38.2	212	40.2	330	39.5
High school diploma*	116	37.5	215	40.8	331	39.6
Post-high school vocational	19	6.1	29	5.5	48	5.7
Junior college degree or more	18	5.8	33	6.3	51	6.1
No data	21	6.8	5	.5	26	3.1
Total	309	100.0	527	100.0	836	100.0

*Including GED (high school equivalency diploma).
Source: Compiled by the authors.

to college degrees). As one might expect, then, Table 4.4 shows that at the time of the interview, the majority of those persons usually in the labor force (about 85 percent of each sample) were unemployed (66.7 percent in Miami, 58.2 percent in Denver). The occupation of those who were then employed was roughly the same, in each city, as their usual occupation, both samples tending to increase in numbers with each decrease in job status level. Although unemployment was higher among the Miami sample, Table 4.5 shows that somewhat fewer Miami than Denver patients were receiving public assistance (27.5 percent versus 35.3 percent). Only about half of each sample, however, had never received public assistance; about 40 percent in each sample were receiving it at the time of the interview or had received it in the two preceding years.

TABLE 4.4

Occupation of Drug-Emergency Patients Interviewed in Two Cities (Respondents Usually in the Labor Force)

	Miami		Denver	
	Number	Percent	Number	Percent
Present	264	100.0	452	100.0
PTMA*	10	3.8	37	8.1
Sales, clerical	23	8.7	27	6.0
Skilled, semiskilled	22	8.3	42	9.3
Unskilled, service	33	12.5	83	18.4
Unemployed	176	66.7	263	58.2
Usual	261	100.0	453	100.0
PTMA	29	11.1	58	12.8
Sales, clerical	61	23.4	68	15.0
Skilled, semiskilled	64	24.5	98	21.6
Unskilled, service	92	35.2	200	44.2
Unemployed	15	5.7	29	5.4

*Professional-technical and management-administrative.
Source: Compiled by the authors.

To summarize, the two samples were similar in having a wide age distribution, over 60 percent whites, generally low education and low-to-middle-status occupations, and a high rate of both unemployment and recourse to public assistance. The primary differences between them were in sex (more females in the Denver sample), age (a slightly greater percentage of older persons in Denver), and minority-group composition (Hispanics outnumbering blacks in the Denver sample, and the reverse in Miami).

TABLE 4.5

Public Assistance History of Drug-Emergency Patients
Interviewed in Two Cities

| | Miami | | Denver | |
	Number	Percent	Number	Percent
Currently receiving	85	27.5	186	35.3
Not now, but:				
Application pending	10	3.2	14	2.7
Did receive in past				
2 years	33	10.7	18	3.4
Did previously	22	7.1	43	8.2
Never received	157	50.8	266	50.5
Unknown	2	.6	--	--
Total	309	100.0	527	100.0

Source: Compiled by the authors.

REASON FOR COMING TO THE HOSPITAL

The most frequent complaint at admission, in both samples, was accidental overdose (38.5 percent of the Miami cases, 54.1 percent of those in Denver). The other major category, as Table 4.6 indicates, was suicide attempts, which accounted for over 20 percent of the cases in each sample. Miami also had a significant number of cases of addiction (including withdrawal cases), particularly as compared to the Denver sample (13.6 percent versus 4.9 percent), as well as more psychotic- or panic-reaction cases (11.0 percent versus 3.6 percent in Denver). These differences between the samples would make one suspect that more narcotic and barbiturate cases would be found in the Miami sample; this is indeed what an examination of primary and secondary substances responsible for admission indicates (see Tables 4.7 and 4.8).

Since Chapter 2 contains a detailed analysis of drug categories involved in drug emergencies, using a better data base for such a discussion than is offered by the interview data, the focus here will be directed toward comparison of the Miami cases with those from the different kind of metropolitan area represented by Denver.

TABLE 4.6

Complaint at Admission of Drug-Emergency Patients
Interviewed in Two Cities

	Miami		Denver	
	Number	Percent	Number	Percent
Suicide attempt	62	20.1	121	23.0
Accidental overdose	119	38.5	285	54.1
Other physical reactions*	8	2.6	32	6.1
Psychotic reaction	34	11.0	19	3.6
Addiction, withdrawal	42	13.6	26	4.9
Infection	12	3.9	13	2.5
Other, unknown	32	10.4	31	5.9
Total	309	100.0	527	100.0

*Allergic reaction, seizure, extrapyramidal reaction.
Source: Compiled by the authors.

In terms of similarities, it should be noted that legally manu-factured and distributed substances account for the clear majority of primary substances responsible for admission; they represent about 60 percent of the Miami cases and about 67 percent of the Denver cases (see Table 4.7). The two samples are also similar in that no secondary substance at all was reported for about half the cases in each sample (see Table 4.8). Where one was reported, however, by far the most prevalent substance was alcohol (18.8 percent in Miami, 20.7 percent in Denver). None of the other spe-cific substance types was involved in even 5 percent of the cases. The differences which do exist for these small case numbers are similar, it might also be noted, to the differences between samples for primary substances--more sedatives in Miami and more over-the-counter and miscellaneous prescription drugs in Denver.

There would seem to be two major differences between the Miami and Denver samples in substance responsible for emergency-room admittance. First, the Miami admissions seem to involve illegal drugs more often. Narcotics alone played either a primary or secondary role in 22.3 percent of the Miami cases, compared to 13.1 percent of those in Denver. The difference for cocaine is even more noticeable--15 cases (4.9 percent) in Miami versus 2 cases (0.4 percent) in Denver. Since Miami is a major city for import and distribution of such drugs, this is not surprising.

TABLE 4.7

Primary Substance Involved for Drug-Emergency
Patients Interviewed in Two Cities

	Miami		Denver	
	Number	Percent	Number	Percent
Minor tranquilizers	47	15.2	133	25.2
Major tranquilizers	21	6.8	28	5.3
Barbiturates	41	13.3	41	7.8
Other sedatives	37	12.0	12	2.3
Unknown sedatives	3	1.0	1	.2
Heroin, opium	50	16.2	35	6.6
Methadone	8	2.6	2	.4
Other narcotics	4	1.3	14	2.7
Analgesics	11	3.6	18	3.4
Miscellaneous prescriptions	10	3.3	48	9.1
Over-the-counter drugs	15	4.9	75	14.2
Antidepressants	5	1.6	8	1.5
Amphetamines	5	1.6	31	5.9
Other stimulants	1	.3	2	.4
Cocaine	7	2.3	2	.4
Marijuana	5	1.6	2	.4
Hallucinogens	6	1.9	26	4.9
Inhalants	4	1.3	2	.4
Poisons	5	1.6	2	.4
Unknown substance	7	2.3	16	3.0
No data	17	5.5	29	5.5
Total	309	100.0	527	100.0

Source: Compiled by the authors.

TABLE 4.8

Secondary Substance Involved for Drug-Emergency
Patients Interviewed in Two Cities

	Miami		Denver	
	Number	Percent	Number	Percent
Minor tranquilizers	16	5.2	18	3.4
Major tranquilizers	2	.6	9	1.7
Barbiturates	9	2.9	14	2.7
Other sedatives	15	4.9	4	.8
Unknown sedatives	--	--	--	--
Heroin, opium	1	.3	4	.8
Methadone	2	.6	1	.2
Other narcotics	5	1.6	13	2.5
Analgesics	1	.3	14	2.7
Miscellaneous prescriptions	7	2.3	25	4.7
Over-the-counter drugs	4	1.3	28	5.3
Alcohol	58	18.8	109	20.7
Antidepressants	3	1.0	5	1.0
Amphetamines	1	.3	12	2.3
Other stimulants	--	--	1	.2
Cocaine	8	2.6	--	--
Marijuana	7	2.3	7	1.3
Hallucinogens	--	--	6	1.1
Inhalants	--	--	--	--
Poisons	2	.6	1	.2
Unknown substance	3	1.0	4	.8
No data	165	53.4	253	48.0
Total	309	100.0	527	100.0

Source: Compiled by the authors.

Second, the Miami admissions seem to involve a higher proportion of the physically addicting drugs--in addition to narcotics,
more antidepressants and fewer over-the-counter drugs. Further,
this would seem to be an even more important difference than the
legal-versus-illicit difference. That is, while there were definitely
more narcotics cases in Miami, if one looks at the less life-
threatening illegal drugs, there is little if any difference between

the samples. Even including cocaine along with marijuana and hallucinogens, the difference for primary substances is 5.9 percent
(Miami) versus 5.7 percent (Denver), and for primary-plus-secondary,
10.7 percent versus 8.2 percent. The marijuana and hallucinogens
alone, then, were involved slightly more often in the Denver cases
than in Miami.

Answers to another interview question also made it quite clear
that the primary substances resulting in an emergency-room experience had been used on a fairly regular basis. As reported in Table
4.9, 51.5 percent of the Miami patients and 42.9 percent of the Denver patients had been using the primary substance on a daily basis.
In addition, in the 217 Miami cases and the 476 Denver cases where
information was available on length of time the primary substance
had been used, 86.6 percent and 67.1 percent of the respective
samples reported using the substance for at least two months prior
to emergency-room admission.

TABLE 4.9

Frequency of Use of the Primary Substance Responsible
for Admission: Drug-Emergency Patients
Interviewed in Two Cities

	Miami		Denver	
	Number	Percent	Number	Percent
Daily	159	51.5	226	42.9
Several times a week	25	8.1	56	10.6
Once a week	12	3.9	24	4.6
Every two weeks	14	4.5	45	8.5
Less than once a month	44	14.2	106	20.1
Does not use	5	1.6	20	3.8
Unknown	50	16.2	50	9.5
Total	309	100.0	527	100.0

Source: Compiled by the authors.

Another major pattern which should be emphasized again is
the predominance of legal drugs in both the Miami and Denver samples. Further, as Table 4.10 indicates, many (and in the case of
Denver, most) of these substances were obtained legitimately. In
Miami, only 22 percent of the primary-substances cases involved

clearly illegal drugs (heroin, cocaine, cannabinols, and hallucinogens), and under half the cases involved drugs reportedly obtained through street, jail, or illegal prescription sources. In Denver, these four illegal drugs accounted for even less of the problem (12.3 percent), and the street/jail/illegal-prescription sources were 23.3 percent of the cases. The biggest drug problem from the point of view of medical emergencies, then, would seem to be legal drugs obtained in legitimate ways.

TABLE 4.10

How the Primary Substance Responsible for Admission
Was Obtained: Drug-Emergency Patients
Interviewed in Two Cities

	Miami		Denver	
	Number	Percent	Number	Percent
Legitimate prescription				
Own	90	29.1	230	43.6
Someone else's	26	8.4	44	8.3
Physician hopping	4	1.3	1	.2
Over-the-counter	12	3.9	65	12.3
Illegal prescription	4	1.3	3	.6
Street	106	34.3	120	22.8
Jail	1	.3	--	--
Other	14	4.5	17	3.2
No data	52	16.8	47	8.9
Total	309	100.0	527	100.0

Source: Compiled by the authors.

To summarize, the two samples were similar in that they indicated (1) a wide range of primary substances as having been responsible for emergency-room admission; (2) a secondary substance in about half the cases (of which roughly 40 percent involved alcohol); and (3) a significant proportion of legally obtained substances. The primary differences between them were that the Miami sample showed a higher percentage of illegal drugs (specifically, heroin and cocaine) as having been responsible for emergency-room admittance and a higher percentage of more dangerous (life-threatening) drugs, even among the legal substances.

GENERAL DRUG-USE PATTERNS

The preceding section suggests that most of the emergency-room drug-reaction patients were not inexperienced in drug use. This is confirmed by the patients' reports on their experience with drug use as summarized in Table 4.11. Over 40 percent of the Miami patients had used one or more of the following: heroin, barbiturates, other sedatives, minor tranquilizers, cocaine, amphetamines, and marijuana or hashish. About 20 percent had used solvents or inhalants, and almost 40 percent had used LSD. In the Denver sample, almost all the percentages for prior drug use were lower--and generally considerably lower--than in the Miami sample. The differences were particularly pronounced for illegal or restricted drugs, where the percentage of Miami patients who reported having used such substances was generally twice that for Denver--or more (as with cocaine--52.1 percent versus 14.4 percent). A similar trend was evident for barbiturates (52.4 percent of the Miami patients, 25.6 percent in Denver), other sedatives (48.2 percent, 21.8 percent), antidepressants (18.8 percent, 8.5 percent), and methadone (29.1 percent, 8.0 percent).

Patterns of current drug use were similar. The Miami sample again had remarkably high reported use, especially for illegal drugs. Over a fourth of the Miami patients, for example, reported current heroin use (26.2 percent), almost as many (24.9 percent) reported current cocaine use, and 50.1 percent reported current marijuana or hashish use. The comparable figures for the Denver sample, however, were 11.6 percent for heroin, 7.4 percent for cocaine, and 26.9 percent for the marijuana. Again, the Miami drug-use figures tended, for all drugs, to be higher than those for Denver; the exception here was analgesics (16.9 percent versus 12.0 percent in Miami). In addition, more current amphetamine use was reported in the Denver sample (17.8 percent versus 11.3 percent), but this is quite possibly a function of the much more frequent use of cocaine in Miami. Similarly, the slightly higher percentage reporting LSD use in Denver (11.6 percent versus 10.0 percent in Miami) seems offset by the lower percentage reporting use of other hallucinogens in Denver (1.9 percent versus 4.2 percent in Miami).

The direction and relative degree of these differences in current drug use between the two samples are generally what one would expect on the basis of the differences between the samples in primary substance responsible for emergency-room admittance (Table 4.7). For example, heroin or opium accounted for 6.6 percent of the Denver admissions--a figure which is about 41 percent of the Miami figure (16.2 percent); one would expect to find, then, that the

TABLE 4.11

Drug–Use Experience of Drug–Emergency Patients Interviewed in Two Cities

| | Ever Used | | | | Currently Using | | | |
| | Miami | | Denver | | Miami | | Denver | |
	Number	Percent	Number	Percent	Number	Percent	Number	Percent
Heroin	143	46.3	97	18.4	81	26.2	58	11.0
Methadone	90	29.1	42	8.0	39	12.6	19	3.6
Other narcotics	119	38.5	93	17.6	41	13.3	45	8.5
Barbiturates	162	52.4	135	25.6	86	27.8	90	17.1
Other sedatives	149	48.2	115	21.8	84	27.2	81	15.4
Minor tranquilizers	181	58.6	236	44.8	111	35.9	178	33.8
Major tranquilizers	86	27.8	84	15.9	37	12.0	55	10.4
Antidepressants	58	18.8	45	8.5	19	6.1	23	4.4
Cocaine	161	52.1	76	14.4	77	24.9	39	7.4
Amphetamines	137	44.3	150	28.5	35	11.3	94	17.8
Other stimulants	35	11.3	11	2.1	11	.4	5	.1
Analgesics	80	25.9	146	27.7	37	12.0	89	16.9
Marijuana	201	65.0	194	36.8	157	50.1	142	26.9
LSD	122	39.5	110	20.9	31	10.0	61	11.6
Other hallucinogens	91	29.4	32	6.1	13	4.2	10	1.9
Solvents, inhalants	61	19.7	29	5.5	15	4.9	7	1.3
Other	12	3.9	68	12.9	9	2.9	62	11.8
Alcohol					229	74.1	427	81.0
Totals	309		527		309		527	

Source: Compiled by the authors.

percentage of Denver patients reporting current use of heroin would bear roughly the same relationship to the comparable Miami figure-- which it does (11.0 percent/26.2 percent = 42.0 percent). There are only two obvious exceptions to this general trend. The largest is for minor tranquilizers, which represent 15.2 percent of the Miami primary-substances reports but 25.2 percent of Denver's--and yet the percentage of each sample using minor tranquilizers is about the same (actually slightly higher in Miami--35.9 percent versus 33.8 percent). A similar situation obtains for hallucinogens--1.9 percent of the primary substances in Miami and 4.9 percent in Denver (1.9 percent versus 6.0 percent when both primary and secondary substances are considered); and yet current use of hallucinogens in the two samples is not that different, and again may actually indicate more use in Miami (10.0 percent for LSD in Miami, 11.6 percent in Denver; others, 4.2 percent in Miami versus 1.9 percent in Denver).

The most obvious possible explanation for these discrepancies is that the two samples could differ in the frequency with which these drugs were being used. Table 4.12 indicates that this was indeed the case for both minor tranquilizers and hallucinogens. While 50.5 percent of the Miami users of minor tranquilizers reported using them daily, 65.2 percent of the Denver users did so; at the other extreme, 27.0 percent of the Miami users reported less-than-weekly use compared to 18.5 percent of the Denver users. With hallucinogens, the difference in daily-use reports is even more marked-- 6.5 percent and 7.7 percent for LSD and other hallucinogens in Miami versus 21.3 percent and 30.0 percent, respectively, in Denver.

It might also be noted in Table 4.12 that for 13 of the 18 drug types listed, daily-use percentages are higher in Denver; and for 13 of 18, less-than-weekly-use percentages are higher in Miami. This looks as if drug use is not only more prevalent in Miami (as indicated by Table 4.11), but also more casual. Finally, the frequency information in Table 4.12 might also be used to explain some of the smaller discrepancies between current-use rates and rates for primary substance involved in hospital admission--but it would seem more satisfactory to go directly to cross-tabulations between frequency of use of a given drug and likelihood of ending up in an emergency room for adverse reactions from that drug.

One other major characteristic of general drug-use patterns covered in the study was the user's age of first use for the various drug types. As Table 4.13 indicates, many of the specific types show highly similar first-use patterns in the two samples. In both samples, for instance, the same four drug types had been used by age 17 by more than 50 percent of those who had ever used the drug: amphetamines, marijuana or hashish, LSD, and solvents or inhalants. The tendency toward first use at an early age is also indicated by the

TABLE 4.12

Frequency of Current Drug Use among Drug-Emergency Patients Interviewed in Two Cities

	Number of Users[a]		Percent Using Daily		Percent Between[b]		Percent Using Less than Weekly	
	Miami	Denver	Miami	Denver	Miami	Denver	Miami	Denver
Heroin	81	58	60.5	44.8	21.0	22.4	18.5	32.8
Methadone	39	19	76.9	84.2	5.1	5.3	17.9	10.5
Other narcotics	41	45	65.9	62.2	9.8	13.3	24.4	24.4
Barbiturates	86	90	48.8	61.1	16.3	17.8	34.9	21.1
Other sedatives	84	81	50.0	64.2	19.0	13.6	31.0	22.2
Minor tranquilizers	111	178	50.5	65.2	22.5	16.3	27.0	18.5
Major tranquilizers	37	55	67.6	70.9	8.1	9.1	24.3	20.0
Antidepressants	19	23	68.4	95.7	21.1	4.3	10.5	.0
Cocaine	77	39	18.2	28.2	35.1	20.5	46.8	51.3
Amphetamines	35	94	37.1	52.1	20.0	16.0	42.9	31.9
Other stimulants	11	5	45.5	40.0	9.1	40.0	45.5	20.0
Analgesics	37	89	45.9	28.1	21.6	23.6	32.4	48.3
Marijuana	157	142	33.8	42.3	36.9	32.4	29.3	25.4
LSD	31	61	6.5	21.3	25.8	21.3	67.7	57.4
Other hallucinogens	13	10	7.7	30.0	23.1	20.0	69.2	50.0
Solvents, inhalants	15	7	40.0	42.9	20.0	57.1	40.0	.0
Other	9	62	55.6	66.1	22.2	6.5	22.2	27.4
Alcohol	229	427	35.8	35.8	28.8	39.1	35.4	25.1

[a]See Table 4.11 for number of users as percentage of total sample.
[b]Percentage using less than daily but at least weekly.
Source: Compiled by the authors.

TABLE 4.13

Age at First Use of Particular Drug Types by Drug-Emergency
Patients Interviewed in Two Cities

	N[a]	% Using, by Age[b] 17	21	25	Median Age	Age by Which 90% Have Used
Miami						
Heroin	143	48.3	80.4	90.9	18	25
Methadone	90	23.3	63.3	80.0	20	30
Other narcotics	119	39.5	68.1	81.5	18	31
Barbiturates	162	46.3	76.5	87.0	18	27
Other sedatives	149	40.3	73.8	85.2	18	30
Minor tranquilizers	181	28.7	59.1	76.8	20	32
Major tranquilizers	86	14.0	47.7	67.4	22	38
Antidepressants	58	10.3	36.2	63.8	23	34
Cocaine	161	34.8	75.2	88.2	19	27
Amphetamines	137	50.4	85.4	93.4	17	24
Other stimulants	35	22.9	62.9	80.0	19	34
Analgesics	80	38.7	62.5	77.5	19	33
Marijuana	201	64.8	86.3	91.8	16	25
LSD	122	50.8	83.6	92.6	17	24
Other hallucinogens	91	44.0	75.8	91.2	18	25
Solvents, inhalants	61	75.4	91.8	93.4	15	21
Denver						
Heroin	97	36.1	74.2	91.8	19	25
Methadone	42	31.0	47.6	73.8	22	34
Other narcotics	93	29.0	52.7	73.1	21	37
Barbiturates	135	43.0	70.4	77.0	19	38
Other sedatives	115	20.9	44.3	62.5	22	46
Minor tranquilizers	236	19.5	40.7	56.4	23	45
Major tranquilizers	84	22.6	56.0	64.3	21	45
Antidepressants	45	13.0	31.1	37.8	30	54
Cocaine	76	34.2	73.7	93.4	19	24
Amphetamines	150	51.3	72.0	87.3	17	26
Other stimulants	11	27.3	45.5	81.8	22	44
Analgesics	146	35.6	56.8	69.9	20	42
Marijuana	194	63.9	84.5	91.2	16	25
LSD	110	62.7	86.4	95.5	17	22
Other hallucinogens	32	46.9	81.3	90.6	18	25
Solvents, inhalants	29	65.5	86.2	89.7	16	23

[a]Number reporting ever using - is 100 percent for the following three
figures. For this number as a percentage of the total sample, see Table 4.11.

[b]For example, 48.3 percent of those who had used heroin had done so by
age 17; 80.4 percent had done so by age 21; and 90.9 percent had done so by age
25 (implying that 9.9 percent reported first use at age 26 or older).

Source: Compiled by the authors.

fact that for both samples, 90 percent of those who had ever used the last three of these drugs (all but the amphetamines) had done so by age 25--which was also the case for both heroin and other hallucinogens besides LSD in both samples, for cocaine in Denver, and for amphetamines in Miami. There was, however, a general tendency for first use to occur somewhat earlier in Miami. Median age at first use was over 20 for only two of the drug types--major tranquilizers and antidepressants--in the Miami subgroups, compared to seven drug types in the Denver subgroups. It is interesting that the specific drug types for which the largest differences between the samples are shown are prescription drugs--specifically, antidepressants, minor tranquilizers, barbiturates, and other sedatives. Median ages at first use are three or more years later in Denver for all but barbiturates; the percentage first using these types after age 25 in Denver is at least 170 percent of the Miami figure for each of the four; and age by which 90 percent of each subgroup has first used is ten to 20 years later in Denver. Differences between the samples on use of illegal drugs, however, tend to be considerably smaller in that they all tend to be first used by age 25 by 90 percent of each subgroup.

To summarize, general drug use among the interviewed emergency-room drug-reaction patients in both samples was quite prevalent in terms of both the patients' having ever used and currently using a wide variety of substances, including illegal drugs. Differences between the samples in general use were generally what one would expect on the basis of differences between them in primary substance responsible for emergency-room admittance, with the exceptions--more admittances but not more use for hallucinogens and minor tranquilizers in Denver--being explainable by more frequent typical use of these two substances among Denver users. For both samples, first use tended to occur at a rather early age, particularly for the illegal drugs--hallucinogens, marijuana, cocaine, and narcotics (especially heroin). The samples were different, however, in that a greater proportion of Miami than Denver patients reported--

- they had previously used most (15 of 17) of the drug types--with particularly pronounced differences for illegal or restricted drugs as well as sedatives and antidepressants;
- they were using the various drug types at the time of the interview (for 14 of 18 types);
- they had lower typical use frequency (for 13 of 18 drug types); and
- they had a tendency toward earlier onset for the prescription drugs--most notably antidepressants, minor tranquilizers, barbiturates, and other sedatives.

PRIOR CONTACT WITH COMMUNITY AGENCIES

Given the relatively high rates of drug use among the emergency-room patients, one might well expect that the majority of the patients would have been in drug treatment programs or at least in an emergency room on some previous occasion. Table 4.14 suggests that this was not necessarily the case. Only about a third of the Miami patients had been in a drug treatment program, and about 18 percent had been in more than one program. The figures for Denver are even lower--16 percent and 3 percent, respectively-- but data could not be obtained for a large percentage of the Denver cases (31.9 percent, compared to under 1 percent in Miami). Table 4.14 also indicates that some of the drug-reaction patients--none of whom, it will be recalled, were in the emergency room due to alcohol as a primary substance--had been in alcohol treatment programs (9.4 percent of the Miami cases and 7.6 percent of those in Denver). Only a few patients reported being in a treatment program at the time of the emergency-room admission.

Prior admission to the emergency room was more comparable for the two samples, as--unfortunately--were the number of no-data cases for this information (which were quite high for both samples). Table 4.14 indicates, however, that 70 of the 250 Miami patients (28.0 percent) from whom information on prior emergency-room admissions could be obtained reported prior admission to the same emergency room--more than half of them (40 of the 70, or 57.1 percent) having been previously admitted two or more times. In Denver, the first figure is quite similar--115 out of 387 (29.7 percent) reporting a prior admission, with even more (81 of the 115, or 70.4 percent) having been previously admitted two or more times.

Larger proportions of the cases reported contact with the criminal justice system. While 107 (34.6 percent) of the Miami patients had been in drug treatment programs, Table 4.15 shows that at least 189 (61.2 percent) had been arrested, at least 135 (43.7 percent) had been arrested in the preceding two years, and at least 123 (39.8 percent) had been convicted. The arrest and conviction figures here are minimum figures, since they all are drawn from tables having more no-data cases than in the treatment infor- mation. The Denver figures are more difficult to compare, because of the high number of no-data cases in treatment information. The 86 patients reporting drug treatment represent only 16.3 percent of the Denver sample; a more accurate figure is probably their per- centage of the 359 cases (24.0 percent) for which drug treatment in- formation is available. The arrest and conviction figures even for the total sample of 527, however, show 270 (51.2 percent) previously arrested, 160 (30.4 percent) arrested in the preceding two years, and 162 (30.7 percent) convicted. These figures represent a very similar treatment-versus-arrest/conviction contrast to that given by the Miami figures.

TABLE 4.14

Prior Drug-Related Treatment Received by Drug-Emergency Patients Interviewed in Two Cities

	Miami		Denver	
	Number	Percent	Number	Percent
Drug treatment programs				
None	198	64.1	275	52.2
One	51	16.5	66	12.5
Two	26	8.4	8	1.5
Three-four	20	6.4	8	1.5
Five or more	10	3.2	2	.3
No data	4	.6	168	31.9
Alcohol treatment programs				
None	270	87.4	301	57.1
One	14	4.5	27	5.1
Two-four	9	2.9	11	2.1
Five or more	6	1.9	2	.4
No data	10	3.2	186	35.3
Prior emergency-room admissions				
None	180	58.3	272	51.6
One	30	9.7	34	6.5
Two	18	5.8	43	8.2
Three-four	15	4.9	16	3.0
Five-seven	5	1.6	11	2.1
Eight or more	2	.6	11	2.1
No data	59	19.1	140	26.6
Total	309	100.0	527	100.0

Source: Compiled by the authors.

TABLE 4.15

Arrests and Convictions of Drug-Emergency Patients
Interviewed in Two Cities

	Miami		Denver	
	Number	Percent	Number	Percent
Total arrests				
None	101	32.7	252	47.8
One	53	17.2	88	16.7
Two-five	76	24.6	94	17.8
Six-ten	29	9.4	40	7.6
Eleven or more	31	10.0	48	9.1
Unknown	19	6.1	5	.9
Arrests in preceding two years				
None	117	37.9	335	63.6
One	67	21.7	90	17.1
Two-five	53	17.2	57	10.8
Six-ten	4	1.3	8	1.5
Eleven or more	11	3.6	5	.9
Unknown	57	18.4	32	6.1
Total convictions				
None	128	41.4	328	62.2
One	57	18.4	86	16.3
Two-five	51	16.5	57	10.8
Six-ten	6	1.9	14	2.7
Eleven or more	9	2.9	5	.9
Unknown	58	18.8	37	7.0
Total	309	100.0	527	100.0

Source: Compiled by the authors.

Table 4.16 shows, furthermore, that many of those arrested were first arrested at an early age. About a fourth of each of the total samples had been arrested by the time they were 17 years of age. By age 24, over half the Miami patients (53.7 percent) and 41.4 percent of the Denver patients had been arrested; these are again percentages for the total samples. As percentages of persons arrested, these figures mean that almost 80 percent of those arrested in each sample had been arrested by the time they were 24 years old.

TABLE 4.16

Age at First Arrest, for Drug-Emergency Patients
Interviewed in Two Cities

| | Miami | | Denver | |
	Number	Percent	Number	Percent
12 and under	13	6.3	26	9.5
13-17	66	31.7	100	36.4
18-24	87	41.8	92	33.5
25-34	23	11.1	41	14.9
35 and over	8	3.8	11	4.0
Unknown	11	5.3	5	1.8
Total arrested*	208	100.0	275	100.0
12 and under	13	4.2	26	4.9
13-17	66	21.4	100	19.0
18-24	87	28.2	92	17.5
25-34	23	7.4	41	7.8
35 and over	8	2.6	11	2.1
Unknown/not applicable	112	36.2	257	48.8
Total sample	309	100.0	527	100.0

*Base = total sample minus persons stating no arrests (see
Table 4.15).
Source: Compiled by the authors.

Table 4.17 indicates that the most common type of crime committed (although not necessarily always resulting in arrest) was, for
both samples, drug crimes. As one would expect from the higher
use rates for illegal drugs in Miami, such crimes were reported by
considerably more of the Miami than Denver patients. While 74.6
percent of the Denver patients said they had not committed any drug
crime, this was true for only 52.4 percent of the Miami patients.
As a percentage of cases with available data, the contrast is even
larger. While 92 of the 254 Miami patients giving such information
admitted at least one drug crime (36.2 percent), this held for only
89 of 482 (18.5 percent) in the Denver sample. The two samples are
also dissimilar on property crimes committed. While 172 out of 251
(31.5 percent) Miami patients giving such information reported at
least one property crime, only 51 of 405 (12.6 percent) did so in the
Denver sample. The figures for personal crimes, however, were

both similar and lower in both samples--40 of 255 (15.7 percent) in Miami and 48 of 404 (11.9 percent) in Denver. It might also be noted that the number of persons reporting the greatest frequency of repeated personal crimes was much lower, in both samples, than the number reporting similarly repeated property or drug crimes. Only three people in the total of 836 reported six or more personal crimes, compared to 22 for property crimes and 24 for drug crimes.

TABLE 4.17

Number of Specific Types of Crimes Committed by Drug-Emergency Patients Interviewed in Two Cities

	Miami		Denver	
	Number	Percent	Number	Percent
Drug crimes				
None	162	52.4	393	74.6
One	46	14.9	54	10.2
Two–five	32	10.4	25	4.7
Six or more	14	4.5	10	1.9
Unknown	55	17.8	45	8.5
Property crimes				
None	172	55.7	354	67.2
One	45	14.6	29	5.5
Two–five	23	7.4	11	2.1
Six or more	11	3.6	11	2.1
Unknown	58	18.8	122	23.1
Crimes against person				
None	215	69.6	356	67.6
One	30	9.7	31	5.9
Two–five	10	3.2	14	2.7
Six or more	0	.0	3	.6
Unknown	54	17.5	123	23.3
Total	309	100.0	527	100.0

Source: Compiled by the authors.

In summary, prior contacts with community agencies were rather similar in both samples. A limited number of the patients in each sample had been in a drug treatment program (about a third of the Miami sample and perhaps a fourth of the Denver sample), a few (8-9 percent) had been in a program for alcohol problems, and about three in ten had been treated in the emergency room before. Relatively few people were in a drug treatment program at the time of the interview. Prior contacts with police and courts were more frequent. In both samples, more persons had been arrested, arrested within the last two years, and even convicted than had previously been enrolled in a drug treatment program. Previous-arrest figures were, in fact, about 175-200 percent of the previous-treatment figures. Further, first arrests tended to take place when the patients were rather young. Finally, for both samples, drug crimes were the most frequently reported type of crime committed, followed by property crimes and, at considerably lower rates, personal crimes. The one major difference between the samples was that both drug and property crimes were reported by about twice as many Miami as Denver patients, although the arrest rates (61.2 percent versus 51.2 percent previously arrested) were not nearly as different from one another.

CHARACTERISTICS OF THREE SELECTED DRUG-EMERGENCY SUBPOPULATIONS

In order to examine the similarity--or difference--between persons coming to the emergency room for adverse reactions to different substances, the three largest drug-type subgroups were targeted. Specifically, details were looked at for persons coming to the emergency room for reactions to (1) minor tranquilizers, (2) sedatives (barbiturates and/or other sedatives), and (3) narcotics (including heroin, methadone, or other narcotics). In both the Miami and Denver samples, many differences between these subgroups appeared in the data.

The first part of Table 4.18 shows the distribution for each of the three subpopulations in the Miami sample by age, sex, race, and ethnicity. In age, the narcotics subgroup was considerably younger than either the sedatives or the minor-tranquilizers subgroup. Only five of the 58 (8.6 percent) narcotics patients were 35 years or over, compared to 15.4 percent of the sedative patients and 27.7 percent of the tranquilizer patients. The sedatives subgroup was the next youngest, since over half these patients were under 24, and the minor-tranquilizers subgroup was clearly the oldest. By sex, differences in the Miami sample were not as large

TABLE 4.18

Basic Demographic Characteristics of Drug-Emergency Patients
Interviewed in Two Cities: Selected Drug Subgroups

	Minor Tranquilizers		Sedatives		Narcotics	
	Number	Percent	Number	Percent	Number	Percent
Miami						
17 and under	4	8.5	4	5.1	0	.0
18-24	15	31.9	37	47.4	21	36.2
25-34	15	31.9	25	32.1	32	55.2
35-49	8	17.0	9	11.5	4	6.9
50 and over	5	10.6	3	3.8	1	1.7
Male	21	44.7	45	57.7	31	53.4
Female	26	55.3	33	42.3	27	46.6
White	32	68.1	63	80.8	26	44.8
Black	4	8.5	6	7.7	28	48.3
Hispanic	9	19.1	9	11.5	3	5.2
Other	2	4.3	0	.0	1	1.7
Total	47	100.0	78	100.0	58	100.0
Denver						
17 and under	3	2.3	0	.0	0	.0
18-24	32	24.1	15	28.3	8	21.6
25-34	52	39.1	20	37.7	24	64.9
35-49	30	22.6	11	20.8	5	13.5
50 and over	16	12.0	6	11.3	0	.0
No data			1	1.9		
Male	49	36.8	25	47.2	27	73.0
Female	84	63.2	28	52.8	10	27.0
White	84	63.2	38	71.7	15	40.5
Black	7	5.3	9	17.0	6	16.2
Hispanic	38	28.6	5	9.4	14	37.8
Other	4	3.0	1	1.9	2	5.4
Total	133	100.0	53	100.0	37	100.0

Source: Compiled by the authors.

as one might expect, although women represented the majority of the tranquilizer cases and men the majority of the narcotics cases (as well as the sedatives cases). In race and ethnicity, the most strik- ing differences were that blacks accounted for almost half the nar- cotics cases (and only 8-9 percent of the other subpopulations), while whites accounted for over 80 percent of the sedatives cases. Both whites and Hispanics accounted for fewer of the narcotics cases than one would expect from their distributions in the sample (about 63 percent and 9 percent, respectively), while blacks represented almost twice as many cases as one would expect by chance (they were 26.5 percent of the Miami interview sample [see Table 4.1] but 48.3 percent of the narcotics cases). Patients coming to the emergency room for both sedative and minor-tranquilizer reactions tended, by contrast, to be white, although it might be noted that Hispanics represented about twice the number of minor-tranquilizer cases one would expect (19.1 percent, compared to their being 9.4 percent of the interview sample).

The demographic distributions of the three drug-type sub- groups in the Denver sample, also shown in Table 4.18, generally reflect even larger differences than the Miami distributions. Here, the predictable sex difference did appear--females accounted for almost two-thirds of the minor-tranquilizer cases, while males ac- counted for almost three-fourths of the narcotics cases. For seda- tives, the two sexes were almost equally distributed. The relative age distributions of the Denver subgroups were also somewhat dif- ferent from those in Miami in that there was little difference between the Denver sedatives and tranquilizers subgroups--both having about 30 percent under age 24, 40 percent in the 25-34 category, and slightly over 30 percent in the 35-plus category. But, as in Miami, the youngest patients were definitely the narcotics-reaction cases, with only 13.5 percent of them being 35 or older. In regard to race and ethnicity, sedative and minor-tranquilizer patients in Denver tended again to be whites, representing about 72 percent and 63 per- cent of these subgroups, respectively. And, again, narcotics patients tended to be minority group members, but here--unlike Miami--they were more likely to be Hispanic (38 percent of the cases) than black (16 percent). Both Hispanics and blacks, however, were overrepre- sented in the narcotics subgroup compared to their representation in the Denver interviews--Hispanics (38 percent versus 25 percent of the sample) only slightly more so than blacks (16 percent versus 12 percent of the sample).

Considering Miami and Denver together, then, the following might be said about each of the drug subpopulations. The typical emergency-room patient with an adverse reaction to a minor tran- quilizer was white, female, and between ages 18 and 35. This contrasts most sharply with the typical narcotics-reaction patients, who were more likely to be male, members of a minority group, and almost always in the 18-to-34 age range. Both age and sex are more difficult to characterize for the sedatives patient, although it can be said that the typical case in the subgroup was--even more certainly than for the tranquilizer cases--more likely to be white.

The information on education and usual occupation for the Miami subgroups given in Table 4.19 suggests that it was the narcotics-reaction patients who were least likely to have graduated from high school and most likely by far to report usual occupations as unskilled or service workers. The typical sedative or minor-tranquilizer patient, on the other hand, was a high-school graduate or more (although it should be noted that over a third of both subgroups did not have a high-school diploma). The most typical occupational-skill level for both--given a breakdown into white-collar versus skilled versus unskilled--was white-collar. However, it is important to note that only the percentages for unskilled workers (including service) were really different for these three Miami subgroups--43.1 percent of the narcotics cases as opposed to 21 percent and 17 percent of the tranquilizer and sedative subgroups, respectively. White-collar workers, surprisingly, made up about as many of the narcotics cases (29 percent) as they did of the other two types (32 percent in each). A related and even more unexpected observation drawn from Table 4.19 is that of the eight college graduates who showed up in these particular Miami subgroups, five were at the emergency room as narcotics cases.

The education and occupation breakdowns for the Denver subgroups, also shown in Table 4.19, are more like what one might expect. On both factors the narcotics patients were more clearly at the bottom--only 5 percent had more than a high-school education, the smallest percentage usually had white-collar occupations, and none of the 19 persons with college degrees who appeared in these subgroups had come to the emergency room as narcotics cases. Still, the education and occupational differences between the three subgroups are not as striking as most of the other subgroup differences. One final observation that can be made on the Denver education/occupation distributions is that the sedatives subgroup is peculiar in having the highest typical education and yet the lowest typical occupation level. Over 20 percent of these patients had some education beyond high school and only about a third had no high-school diploma, and yet almost half of them fell into the unskilled-service and usually-unemployed categories.

Again looking for common patterns in the two samples, it can be stated that differences on education and usual occupation between these three drug-type subgroups are not as large as one might expect,

TABLE 4.19

Educational Attainment and Usual Occupation of Drug-Emergency Patients
Interviewed in Two Cities: Selected Drug Subgroups

	Minor Tranquilizers		Sedatives		Narcotics	
	Number	Percent	Number	Percent	Number	Percent
Miami						
Education						
Less than high school	18	38.3	29	37.2	27	46.6
High school, GED[a]	21	44.7	33	42.3	23	39.7
Some beyond high school	3	6.4	9	11.5	2	3.4
College	0	.0	3	3.8	5	8.6
No data	5	10.6	4	5.1	1	1.7
Usual occupation						
PTMA[b]	3	6.4	9	11.5	7	12.1
Sales, clerical	12	25.5	16	20.5	10	17.2
Skilled, semiskilled	7	14.9	23	29.5	11	19.0
Unskilled, service	10	21.3	13	16.7	25	43.1
Unemployed, other	1	2.1	7	9.0	2	3.4
Housewife	2	4.3	4	5.1	1	1.7
Student	6	12.8	3	3.8	0	.0
No data	6	12.8	3	3.8	2	3.4
Total	47	100.0	78	100.0	58	100.0
Denver						
Education						
Less than high school	57	42.9	18	34.0	17	45.9
High school, GED	53	39.8	22	41.5	18	48.6
Some beyond high school	10	7.5	3	5.7	2	5.4
College degree	11	8.3	8	15.1	0	.0
Usual occupation						
PTMA	76	12.0	7	13.2	4	10.8
Sales, clerical	24	18.0	7	13.2	3	8.1
Skilled, semiskilled	26	19.5	8	15.1	12	32.4
Unskilled, service	38	28.6	22	41.5	14	37.8
Unemployed, other	13	9.8	4	7.5	0	.0
Housewife	10	7.6	2	3.8	2	5.6
Student	4	3.1	3	5.7	1	2.8
Total	133	100.0	53	100.0	37	100.0

[a]High school equivalency diploma.
[b]Professional-technical and management-administrative.
Source: Compiled by the authors.

but the differences which do exist tend to show that the narcotics patients were less likely to have a high-school diploma, any education beyond high school, or a white-collar job as the usual occupation, than were the sedatives or minor-tranquilizers patients.

When the three drug-type subgroups are compared on characteristic-use patterns, a definite trend can be seen in these data. In terms of length of use of the drug in question, frequency of use, age at first use, and how the drug was obtained, the trend in severity of apparent problem ran from narcotics (most severe) to sedatives to minor tranquilizers.

This holds fairly well for both the Miami and the Denver samples, as shown in Table 4.20. In terms of median length of use, for example, the trend in Miami (narcotics-sedatives-tranquilizers) ran from four years to one year to half a year; in Denver, it ran from five to three to one. In terms of percentage using each drug type for more than a year, the Miami figures were 79 percent-49 percent-36 percent, and those for Denver were 78 percent-57 percent-41 percent--again, for narcotics-sedatives-tranquilizers. For frequency of use, the Miami less-than-weekly use percentages were 3 percent-18 percent-25.5 percent, but the Denver differences did not follow the same trend, since they were 30 percent-21 percent-24 percent. In fact, the Denver percentages using each drug type daily were the opposite of what one might expect--38 percent-53 percent-60 percent (that is, 60 percent of the minor-tranquilizer patients but only 38 percent of the narcotics patients were using these respective drugs daily--compared to Miami's 60 percent and 83 percent, respectively). This would lead one to suspect that there was a difference between the Denver and Miami narcotics subgroups in how the drugs were obtained--which is borne out by Table 4.20. While 17 percent of the Miami narcotics patients said they obtained the drug legally, this was the case for only one (2.7 percent) of the Denver narcotics patients. Since Table 4.21 indicates that there is little if any difference between these two subgroups in type of narcotic used, one must conclude that there was a bigger street market for methadone and other narcotics in Denver, or that these drugs were easier to obtain legally in Miami. In any case, the higher frequency of use in Miami was accompanied by figures indicating greater success in obtaining narcotics legally in Miami.

Returning to the narcotic-sedative-tranquilizer trend, the other information in Table 4.20 again generally reflects the same relationships. The Miami figures for cases with first use by age 17, for example, were 38 percent-32 percent-19 percent, and those in Denver were 30 percent-23 percent-13.5 percent--with first use after age 34 indicating the same general pattern in both samples. Finally, the biggest differences between the three drug types are shown in the information on how the drug was obtained. In Miami, the percentages (for narcotics-sedatives-tranquilizers) obtaining these drugs on the street were 76 percent–41 percent–15 percent, while in Denver, the respective figures were 92 percent–34 percent–8 percent--both trends indicating a majority of the sedatives patients and the overwhelming majority of the minor-tranquilizers patients obtained the drug that brought them to the emergency room through prescriptions (which, the data indicate, most often were their own legitimate prescriptions).

The same relative position of the three drug-type subgroups-- narcotics, then sedatives, then minor tranquilizers--also appears when one looks at how involved these patients were in multiple-drug use. Again, although the amount of drug use for all three subgroups was generally higher in Miami than Denver, Table 4.21 shows that in both Miami and Denver, polydrug use was most frequent among the narcotics patients and least frequent among the minor-tranquilizer patients. Computation of the average number of current-drug-use reports for each of the Miami subgroups shows the narcotics subgroup had an average of 3.69 reports (214 current-use reports, for 58 people), compared to 3.51 for sedatives and 2.45 for minor tranquilizers. The comparable figures for Denver were 2.89, 2.25, and 2.03. Even computing average reports of current use of substances not in the same drug category, the Miami narcotics-sedatives-tranquilizers figures were 2.38, 2.32, and 1.79; for the Denver sample, they were 1.68, 1.25, and 1.20.

Table 4.21 also provides some information on which particular other drugs were most likely to be used by each drug-type subgroup. For the Miami narcotics-reaction patients, for example, Table 4.21 shows that not only did at least 15 percent of the sample use each of the three narcotics types, but at least the same number also reported using barbiturates (19 percent), other sedatives (19 percent), methadone (33 percent), minor tranquilizers (36 percent), major tranquilizers (17 percent), cocaine (44.8 percent), and marijuana or hashish (58.6 percent). A similar list for the Miami sedatives patients would omit only methadone and major tranquilizers; but for the Miami minor-tranquilizer patients, there would be listed, besides minor tranquilizers, only barbiturates, other sedatives, and cocaine (all at 15 percent) and the cannabinols (45 percent).

The number of current-use reports for specific drugs at this arbitrary cutoff point (15 percent) was generally smaller for the Denver subgroups. Still, among narcotics patients, there were quite a few current users of minor tranquilizers (43 percent), as well as a 15 percent-or-better rate for barbiturates (16 percent), amphetamines (16 percent), and marijuana or hashish (27 percent). For sedatives patients in Denver, only minor tranquilizers (26 percent) and the cannabinols (15 percent) had this many reports of

TABLE 4.20

Characteristics of Use of Drug Responsible for Admission of Drug-Emergency
Patients Interviewed in Two Cities: Selected Drug Subgroups

	Minor Tranquilizers		Sedatives		Narcotics	
	Number	Percent	Number	Percent	Number	Percent
Miami						
I. Length of use						
2 months or less	13	27.7	22	28.2	4	6.9
3-12 months	13	27.7	18	23.1	5	8.6
1.25-3.50 years	13	27.7	19	24.4	18	31.0
4 or more years	4	8.5	14	17.9	28	48.3
No data	4	8.5	5	6.4	3	5.2
(Median)[a]	(6 mos.)		(12 mos.)		(4 years)	
II. Frequency of use						
Daily	28	59.6	39	50.0	48	82.8
Once-several times/week	5	10.6	14	17.9	6	10.3
Less than weekly	12	25.5	14	17.9	2	3.4
No data	2	4.3	11	14.1	2	3.4
III. Age at first use						
17 or under	9	19.1	25	32.1	22	37.9
18-24	20	42.6	31	39.7	26	44.8
25-34	8	17.0	7	9.0	7	12.1
35 or more	8	17.0	8	10.3	0	.0
No data	2	4.3	7	9.0	3	5.2
(Median)[a]	(22)		(19)		(19)	
IV. How obtained						
Own legal Rx	27	57.4	21	26.9	10[b]	17.2
Other Rx	7	14.9	14	17.9	0	.0
Street	7	14.9	32	41.0	44	75.9
Other, no data	6	12.8	11	14.1	4	6.9
Total	47	100.0	78	100.0	58	100.0

Denver

I. Length of use					
2 months or less	47	35.3	12	22.6	4	10.8
3-12 months	29	21.8	9	17.0	3	8.1
1.25-3.50 years	24	18.0	5	9.4	5	13.5
4 or more years	30	22.6	25	47.2	24	64.9
No data	3	2.3	2	3.8	1	2.7
(Median)[a]	(12 mos.)		(3 years)		(5 years)	
II. Frequency of use					
Daily	80	60.2	28	52.8	14	37.8
Once-several times/week	19	14.3	11	20.8	9	24.3
Less than weekly	32	24.1	11	20.8	11	29.7
No data	2	1.5	3	5.7	3	8.1
III. Age at first use					
17 or under	18	13.5	12	22.6	11	29.7
18-24	38	28.6	20	37.7	20	54.1
25-34	40	30.1	6	11.3	4	10.8
35 or more	37	27.8	12	22.6	2	5.4
No data	0	.0	3	5.5	0	.0
(Median)[a]	(27)		(21)		(20)	
IV. How obtained					
Own legal Rx	105	78.9	26	49.1	1	2.7
Other Rx	14	10.5	7	13.2	0	.0
Street	10	7.5	18	34.0	34	91.9
Other, no data	4	3.0	2	3.8	2	5.4
Total	133	100.0	53	100.0	37	100.0

[a]For available data.
[b]Includes two over-the-counter drugs.
Source: Compiled by the authors.

TABLE 4.21

Current Drug Use of Drug-Emergency Patients Interviewed
in Two Cities: Selected Drug Subgroups

	Minor Tranquilizers		Sedatives		Narcotics	
	Number	Percent	Number	Percent	Number	Percent
Miami						
Heroin	5	10.6	15	19.2	(48	82.8)
Methadone	3	6.4	10	12.8	(19	32.8)
Other narcotics	5	10.6	13	16.7	(9	15.5)
Barbiturates	7	14.9	(47	60.3)	11	19.0
Other sedatives	7	14.9	(46	59.0)	11	19.0
Minor tranquilizers	(31	66.0)	28	35.9	21	36.2
Major tranquilizers	5	10.6	4	5.1	10	17.2
Antidepressants	2	4.3	5	6.4	2	3.4
Cocaine	7	14.9	22	28.2	26	44.8
Amphetamines	6	12.8	5	6.4	7	12.1
Other stimulants	1	2.1	4	5.1	3	5.2
Analgesics	4	8.5	10	12.8	3	5.2
Marijuana or hashish	21	44.7	50	64.1	34	58.6
LSD	6	12.8	7	9.0	4	6.9
Other hallucinogens	2	4.3	1	1.3	3	5.2
Solvents-inhalants	3	6.4	4	5.1	2	3.4
Other	0	.0	3	3.8	1	1.7
Total	47		78		58	
Denver						
Heroin	9	6.8	4	7.5	(31	83.8)
Methadone	3	2.3	1	1.9	(9	24.3)
Other narcotics	11	8.3	2	3.8	(5	13.5)
Barbiturates	15	11.3	(34	64.2)	6	16.2
Other sedatives	18	13.5	(19	35.8)	1	2.7
Minor tranquilizers	(110	82.7)	14	26.4	16	43.2
Major tranquilizers	7	5.3	6	11.3	3	8.1
Antidepressants	5	3.8	2	3.8	2	5.4
Cocaine	7	5.3	5	9.4	5	13.5
Amphetamines	13	9.8	6	11.3	6	16.2
Other stimulants	1	.8	0	.0	1	2.7
Analgesics	20	15.0	3	5.7	4	10.8
Marijuana or hashish	28	21.1	8	15.1	10	27.0
LSD	11	8.3	4	7.5	5	13.5
Other hallucinogens	2	1.5	0	.0	1	2.7
Solvents-inhalants	2	1.5	0	.0	0	.0
Other	8	6.0	11	20.8	2	5.4
Total	133		53		37	

Note: Totals add to more than 100 percent due to multiple responses.
Source: Compiled by the authors.

66

current use, and for Denver minor-tranquilizers patients, the only drug types at this level were marijuana or hashish (21 percent) and analgesics (15 percent).

And yet, Table 4.22 shows that very few of the patients in either sample were in drug treatment at the time of their appearance at the emergency room. Narcotics-reaction patients were the most likely to have been treated or to be in treatment; but even for this subgroup, 40 percent of the Miami narcotics patients and eight of the 23 Denver patients for whom data were available (34 percent) said they had never been in a drug treatment program. The smallest numbers reporting past or current treatment were for the minor-tranquilizer patients--only 19 percent of the Miami subgroup and 20 percent of the Denver subgroup reported being or having been in a drug treatment program. And, as with many of the other factors in this analysis, the sedatives patients came out, in both samples, somewhere between the other two subgroups.

Finally, the same pattern also generally appears in regard to arrests, first arrests at an early age, convictions, and crimes committed. For example, Table 4.23 shows the Miami narcotics-sedatives-tranquilizer percentages for patients previously arrested at 86 percent-69 percent-51 percent; the parallel figures for Denver are 92 percent-55 percent-45 percent. Finally, it might also be noted that in this table, as well as many of the previous ones, for Miami the percentages for sedatives cases tended to be closer to those for the narcotics patients, while for Denver, percentages for sedatives patients tended to look more like those for the minor-tranquilizer cases.

SUMMARY

The preliminary analysis of these Miami and Denver interview data suggest much relative to drug-emergency patients. In summary, 309 acute drug-reactions patients in Miami and 527 in Denver were interviewed during the latter part of 1975 and early 1976. These individuals were typically whites under the age of 35, more than half of whom had finished high school, and were unemployed at the time of interviewing. The majority of these patients had come to the attention of the hospital emergency rooms due to suicide attempts or accidental overdoses, and the substances involved in these acute reactions were overwhelmingly legally manufactured and distributed drugs. These individuals had been using the drug in question at least several times a week, they were involved with a variety of other substances, and had begun their drug-using careers during adolescence. Finally, the majority of these patients had not previously

TABLE 4.22

Prior Drug Treatment Received by Drug-Emergency Patients Interviewed in Two Cities: Selected Drug Subgroups

	Minor Tranquilizers		Sedatives		Narcotics	
	Number	Percent	Number	Percent	Number	Percent
Miami						
I. Drug treatment programs						
Never	37	78.7	48	61.5	23	39.7
Before–not now	7	14.9	23	29.5	25	43.1
Currently in	2	4.3	7	9.0	10	17.2
No data	1	2.1	0	.0	0	.0
Total	47	100.0	78	100.0	58	100.0
II. Alcohol treatment programs						
Never	39	83.0	64	82.1	52	89.7
Before–not now	3	6.4	5	6.4	1	1.7
Currently in	1	2.1	3	3.8	0	.0
No data	4	8.5	6	7.7	5	8.6
Total	47	100.0	78	100.0	58	100.0
Denver						
I. Drug treatment programs						
Never	69	51.9	24	45.3	8	21.6
Before–not now	22	16.5	13	24.5	11	29.7
Currently in	4	3.0	1	1.9	4	10.8
No data	38	28.6	15	28.3	14	37.8
Total	133	100.0	53	100.0	37	100.0
II. Alcohol treatment programs						
Never	77	57.9	27	50.9	12	32.4
Before–not now	9	6.8	5	9.4	4	10.8
Currently in	1	.7	1	1.9	1	2.7
No data	46	34.6	20	37.7	20	54.1
Total	133	100.0	53	100.0	37	100.0

Source: Compiled by the authors.

TABLE 4.23

Crime and Criminal Justice Involvement of Drug-Emergency Patients
Interviewed in Two Cities: Selected Drug Subgroups

	Minor Tranquilizers		Sedatives		Narcotics	
	Number	Percent	Number	Percent	Number	Percent
Miami						
Ever arrested	24	51.1	54	69.2	50	86.2
Arrested by age 17	11	23.4	24	30.8	14	24.1
Arrested by age 25	20	42.6	48	61.5	42	72.4
Ever convicted	10	21.3	34	43.6	29	50.0
Crime committed						
Drug	11	23.4	32	41.0	21	36.2
Property	11	23.4	22	28.2	27	46.6
Personal	3	6.4	11	14.1	7	12.1
Total	47		78		58	
Denver						
Ever arrested	60	45.1	29	54.7	34	91.9
Arrested by age 17	20	15.0	13	24.5	24	64.9
Arrested by age 25	47	35.3	25	47.2	33	89.2
Ever convicted	30	22.6	20	37.7	24	64.9
Crime committed						
Drug	14	10.5	9	17.0	23	62.2
Property	13	9.8	6	11.3	8	21.6
Personal	7	5.3	3	5.7	7	18.9
Total	133		53		37	

*Due to multiple categories, items add to more than 100 percent.
Source: Compiled by the authors.

received any formal treatment for drug-abuse problems, but more than half had histories of arrest.

Some significant differences within this population emerged through an examination of those patients whose drug reactions had involved minor tranquilizers, sedatives, and narcotics. The tranquilizer patients were primarily white females under age 35. They had been using these drugs on a daily basis and had obtained them legally, and they were not overly involved with many other drugs. Most of these individuals had never received any drug treatment, but slightly more than half had been arrested, usually after age 18. By contrast, while the narcotics patients were only slightly older than the minor-tranquilizer patients, they were more often males and of minority group membership. They were overwhelmingly daily or several-times-weekly users, had begun using drugs prior to age 25, and obtained their drugs illegally. In addition, these narcotics cases were more heavily involved with other drugs, significant proportions had never been in treatment, and most had been previously arrested. The sedative cases emerged as a cross section of the tranquilizer and narcotics cases.

What these data reveal is that clearly alternative types of drug users are coming to the attention of hospital emergency rooms. The minor-tranquilizer patient appears to be an individual only minimally involved with drugs, but who gets into trouble with drugs through medicine misuse or self-medication. These individuals have rarely received treatment for their drug taking, likely the result of the unavailability of programs geared to their needs. In contrast, the narcotics patients resemble the typical populations found in formal drug treatment programs. However, these data suggest that significant numbers of these individuals have not come to the attention of drug programs, and that the emergency room may have been their first treatment contact. This would suggest that for a portion of the narcotics-using population, emergency-room data may indeed have utility for predicting what the upcoming treatment program populations may look like.

5

A COMPARISON OF DRUG-EMERGENCY
PATIENTS AND DRUG-PROGRAM CLIENTS

The two preceding chapters describe in some detail the major
demographic and social characteristics of drug-emergency patients
in Dade County, particularly those patients seen at the emergency
room of the county's only public hospital, Jackson Memorial. One
theme which runs throughout both these chapters is the rather surprising relationship between drug emergencies and drug treatment.
Specifically, Chapter 3 reports that under 6 percent of the drug-
emergency patients seen at Jackson Memorial Hospital—and under
1 percent of the drug-emergency patients treated at other hospitals
—were referred to a drug program after being treated for the crisis
situation (see Table 3.5). And, focusing on patient as well as hospital actions, Chapter 4 reports that almost two-thirds of the Jackson
Memorial drug-emergency patients who were interviewed indicated
that they had never been in a drug treatment program of any kind
(see Table 4.14). Given the rather extensive experiences with both
licit and illicit drug use also reported in Chapter 4 as being typical
of many of the drug-emergency patients, these figures indicate a
surprising degree of discontinuity between emergency-room treatment for drug reactions and drug-program treatment for drug abuse.
This is not to say, of course, that all adverse drug reactions are
due to drug abuse. Rather, the argument being made here is that
the general patterns of drug use displayed by the drug-emergency
patients (as indicated by the interview data reported in Chapter 4)
is such that drug misuse can be given blame for at least a substantial proportion of the adverse-reaction crises seen at Jackson
Memorial. Accordingly, it seems appropriate to inquire as to why
so few drug-emergency patients were referred to drug treatment
programs, why so few reported prior drug-program treatment experience, and what the difference is between drug-emergency-
patient populations and drug-program-client populations. These
questions represent the topic explored in this chapter.

The data base representing drug-emergency patients is the same one discussed at length in the last chapter: 309 interviews with drug-emergency patients at Jackson Memorial Hospital done between August 1975 and April 1976. The information on drug-program clients, however, comes from a different kind of interview, done at the central intake unit of the Dade County Comprehensive Drug Program (CDP). This program and the client interviews are described below, followed by an analysis of the differences between the emergency-patient and program-client populations.

THE DADE COUNTY COMPREHENSIVE DRUG PROGRAM

In Dade County the vast majority of services directed toward the drug-abusing population are conducted under the auspices of the Comprehensive Drug Program. The CDP was established in 1971 by the National Institute of Mental Health (NIMH) as an umbrella organization to provide drug treatment on a countywide basis by coordinating the then-existing treatment programs so as to best utilize the community's resources and facilities.

The CDP services were organized in the multimodality tradition of NIMH, offering five basic types of treatment: detoxification, five outpatient clinics, four methadone maintenance facilities, six daytime-only therapeutic communities, and nine fully residential therapeutic communities. Before entering one of these specific programs, however, all clients are interviewed at a central intake office. Data used in discussing treatment program clients in this chapter are derived from a set of these intake interviews.

All of the 1,302 CDP intake interviews done between January 1 and June 20, 1974 were analyzed and used for this study. Although the interview instrument used by the CDP was somewhat different from the question schedule used with the emergency-room patients, both contained basic social, drug-use, and arrest-history items. The content and organization of the two data bases were thus similar enough to permit comparison of the two drug-problem populations.

FINDINGS

The sex ratio of acute drug-reaction emergency-room patients and treatment-program clients appears in Table 5.1. As usually found in profiles of drug users, three out of every four treatment clients (76.0 percent) were male. In contrast, about one-half of the emergency-room patients (52.4 percent) were male. The considerably larger proportion of women in this patient sample makes that group clearly different from the population of drug users in treatment programs.

TABLE 5.1

Basic Demographic Characteristics of Drug-Emergency Patients and Drug-Program Clients

	Drug-Emergency Patients		Drug-Program Clients	
	Number	Percent	Number	Percent
Male	162	52.4	990	76.0
Female	147	47.6	303	23.3
Unknown	—	—	9	.7
White	193	62.5	525	40.3
Hispanic	29	9.4	94	9.2
Black	82	26.5	658	50.5
Other	5	1.6	25	1.9
17 years and under	10	3.2	63	4.8
18-24 years	118	38.2	569	43.7
25-34 years	117	37.9	554	42.5
35-49 years	42	13.6	96	7.4
50-98 years and above	22	7.1	9	.7
Unknown	0	.0	11	.8
Total	309	100.0	1,302	100.0

Source: Compiled by the authors.

The racial and ethnic composition of drug users in treatment programs and the acute drug-reaction emergency-room patients also appears in Table 5.1. Hispanic persons were underrepresented in both drug-using populations. Although persons of Hispanic heritage constituted approximately one-third of the Dade County population in 1973, considerably fewer were present in either the patient (9.4 percent) or treatment (7.2 percent) groups. Most research has noted that blacks are overrepresented in the drug-using population. Therefore, we expected that there would be a greater proportion of

blacks in treatment programs than in the hospital sample—a prediction which was clearly supported by these data. However, when
contrasted to their proportional representation with the Dade County
population (15.0 percent), black overrepresentation exists for both
the emergency room's drug-related patients (26.5 percent) and the
treatment clients (50.5 percent). This modest overrepresentation
of blacks among the acute drug-reaction patients may be related
to this group's perception of the function of the emergency room.
Since the use of emergency-room services is not uniform across
all demographic groups (Duff and Hollingshead 1968, p. 111; Berman
and Luck 1971), it is likely that blacks, due to their proximity to
the hospital and the nature of private medical care in their communities, are more likely than other racial or ethnic groups to utilize
the emergency room as their primary health care facility. The
fact remains that approximately one out of four emergency-room
patients is black, while one in two treatment-program clients is
black. While the majority of drug-emergency patients were white
(62.5 percent), less than one-half (40.2 percent) of the program
clients were white.

The age distribution of these two groups (Table 5.1) indicates
that the emergency-room patients tended to be somewhat older than
their treatment-program counterparts. In contrast to the 8.1 percent of the treatment clients who were at least 35 years of age, 20.7
percent of the hospital patients were of this age group. However, the
18-to-24 age cohort was the modal category for both the emergency-
room (38.2 percent) and the drug-treatment-program respondents
(44.1 percent). The sizable concentration of respondents in this
age group is similar to what has been observed by others regarding
the relative youthfulness of drug users in treatment.

The social status of the treatment-program clients and the
emergency-room patients can be approximated by their educational
and occupational achievement levels. As Table 5.2 indicates, the
emergency-room patients had generally completed more education
than had the treatment-program clients. Although only a few (5.5
percent) emergency patients reported less than an eighth-grade education, one in every four treatment-program clients did not have
a grade-school diploma. Similarly, while 11.9 percent of the
emergency-room group had some post-high-school education, only
6.9 percent of the treatment clients reported any post-high-school
training.

The emergency-room patients also were more likely to be
employed and to work in higher-status occupations than the drug
treatment clients. Table 5.3 indicates that the emergency-room
patients were about twice as likely to hold white-collar positions
(10.6 percent, versus 5.2 percent for the treatment clients). Both

TABLE 5.2

Educational Attainment of Drug-Emergency
Patients and Drug-Program Clients

	Drug-Emergency Patients		Drug-Program Clients	
	Number	Percent	Number	Percent
Less than eighth grade	17	5.5	327	25.1
Grade school diploma	118	38.2	346	26.6
High school or GED*	116	37.5	516	39.6
Vocational-technical	19	6.1	50	3.8
Jr. college or more	18	5.8	40	3.1
Unknown	21	6.8	23	1.8
Total	309	100.0	1,302	100.0

*High school equivalency diploma.
Source: Compiled by the authors.

TABLE 5.3

Present Occupation of Drug-Emergency
Patients and Drug-Program Clients

	Drug-Emergency Patients		Drug-Program Clients	
	Number	Percent	Number	Percent
PTMA*	10	3.2	25	1.9
Clerical	23	7.4	43	3.3
Skilled/semiskilled	22	7.1	133	10.2
Unskilled	33	10.7	125	9.6
Unemployed	176	57.0	926	71.1
Housewife/student	44	14.2	40	3.1
Unknown	1	.3	10	.8
Total	309	100.0	1,302	100.0

*Professional-technical and management-administrative.
Source: Compiled by the authors.

populations had an extremely high unemployment rate—over half the emergency-room patients and nearly three-fourths of the treatment clients were unemployed. Finally, emergency-room patients (14.2 percent) were more likely than treatment clients (3.1 percent) to be housewives or students.

Data presented in Table 5.4 reflect the differences in the types of drugs which the treatment-program clients reported as their primary drug of abuse and the drugs which were responsible for emergency-room admissions. The drug categories were ordered from those drugs historically considered most problematic by official law enforcement opinion (heroin, cocaine, hallucinogens), to those substances that have received some official attention but, overall, have a more moderate social-problem image (stimulants, sedatives, and tranquilizers), to other associated substances to which legal sanctions have given comparatively little attention (miscellaneous substances, for example, antibiotics, over-the-counter substances).

Table 5.4 indicates that definite differences in drugs used exist between the emergency-room and the treatment-program groups. Heroin was the drug of choice for 58.1 percent of the treatment-program clients, a mirror of what other researchers have found when other program-client groups have been studied. In sharp contrast, only 16.2 percent of the emergency-room patients entered the hospital with a heroin-connected problem. Although small in percentage of primary substance involved, cocaine was also more likely to be used by the treatment population (3.8 percent) than to be the primary drug problem for emergency-room patients (2.3 percent). Hallucinogens, another category of substances which has received widespread official concern, were cited as the primary substance of use by 14.6 percent of the program clients but by only 3.6 percent of the emergency-room patients. On the other hand, sedative and tranquilizer use, while mentioned by only 5.3 percent of the treatment-program clients, was involved in almost half (48.2 percent) of all drug-emergency cases. The use of miscellaneous drugs for medical purposes or of over-the-counter products was similarly more often reported by the emergency-room patients (most of the 11.3 percent shown in the "other" category) than by the drug-treatment clients (1.2 percent). Thus, while four out of every five treatment clients used drugs that have been the principal objects of legal control (heroin, cocaine, hallucinogens), only 22.1 percent of the emergency-room clients reported that any of these substances were primary elements of their acute drug reactions.

Closely associated with the discussion of one's principal drug of use is the question of how the user obtained this substance. These data are presented in Table 5.5. Over 40 percent of the

TABLE 5.4

Primary Substance Involved for Drug-Emergency
Patients and Drug-Program Clients

	Drug-Emergency Patients		Drug-Program Clients	
	Number	Percent	Number	Percent
Heroin	50	16.2	756	58.1
Cocaine	7	2.3	49	3.8
Hallucinogens and marijuana	11	3.6	190	14.6
Inhalants	4	1.3	10	.8
Stimulants	6	1.9	21	1.6
Narcotics and analgesics	23	7.4	77	5.9
Sedatives and tranquilizers	149	48.2	69	5.3
Other	35	11.3	15	1.2
Unknown	24	7.8	115	8.8
Total	309	100.0	1,302	100.0

Source: Compiled by the authors.

TABLE 5.5

How the Primary Substance Responsible for Admission
Was Obtained: Drug-Emergency Patients and
Drug-Program Clients

	Drug-Emergency Patients		Drug-Program Clients	
	Number	Percent	Number	Percent
Legal prescription or clinic	115	37.2	54	4.1
Illegal prescription	4	1.3	11	.8
Legal patent medicine purchase	12	3.9	4	.3
Illegal street purchase, theft, hustle	126	40.8	1,067	82.0
Unknown	52	16.8	166	12.7
Total	309	100.0	1,302	100.0

Source: Compiled by the authors.

drug-emergency patients but only about 5 percent of the program clients obtained their substances through legal prescription, clinic, or over-the-counter purchases. By contrast, most program clients (82 percent) utilized illegal street sources in securing their drug supply. Given the previously reported information on which drugs are likeliest to be involved for the two populations, these figures are not surprising. The unexpected figure, however, is the percentage of hospital patients obtaining drugs from illegal sources (40.8 percent). This is a higher percentage than one might predict solely on the basis of how many of the drug-emergency cases involved illicit drugs (22.1 percent). The difference may well be attributable to the 35 percent of drug-emergency patients who were then or had been drug-program clients (see Table 4.14), since street sources are obviously the usual mode of securing drugs for this population. Nonetheless, in comparing those two populations, it should be kept in mind that the biggest difference shown in Table 5.5 is that the emergency patients were some eight times likelier than the program clients (40 percent versus 5 percent) to obtain the drug involved in their problem from legal sources.

Table 5.6 suggests that another difference between these populations is that the treatment-program clients tended to be younger than the drug-emergency patients when they first used the primary drug responsible for their admission to the program or the emergency room. More than 60 percent of the program clients first used the drug in question between the ages of 13 and 21, whereas less than half (42.7 percent) of the emergency-room patients reported that their use began at a comparable age. Further, the emergency-room patients were about three times likelier (13.6 percent versus 4.2 percent) to be 30 years old or more at the time they first used the drug.

To compare the two populations in terms of criminal involvement, answers were condensed from respondents' self-reports on number and dates of arrests, if any. Table 5.7 shows that prior to initial drug use, relatively few emergency-room patients (15.2 percent) or treatment-program clients (10.4 percent) had ever been arrested for any reason other than a traffic violation.

A very different picture emerges, however, when the two groups are compared in terms of their arrest histories after beginning drug use (also shown in Table 5.7). Both populations had very high arrest rates after the onset of drug use, and the rates were particularly high for the treatment-program clients. Almost 45 percent of the drug-emergency patients had been arrested at least once by the time they came to the emergency room—three times the percentage reporting arrests prior to initial drug use. But treatment-program clients reported even a higher rate of arrests;

TABLE 5.6

Age at First Use of Primary Substance Responsible for
Admission: Drug-Emergency Patients and
Drug-Program Clients

	Drug-Emergency Patients		Drug-Program Clients	
	Number	Percent	Number	Percent
Pre-teen	11	3.6	48	3.7
13-17 years	61	19.7	409	31.4
18-21 years	71	23.0	390	30.0
22-25 years	53	17.2	153	11.8
26-29 years	21	6.8	74	5.7
30 years and above	42	13.6	55	4.2
Unknown	50	16.2	173	13.3
Total	309	100.0	1,302	100.0

Source: Compiled by the authors.

TABLE 5.7

Arrest History Relative to Initial Drug Use for
Drug-Emergency Patients and
Drug-Program Clients

	Drug-Emergency Patients		Drug-Program Clients	
	Number	Percent	Number	Percent
Before Beginning Drug Use				
Never arrested	250	80.9	1,128	86.6
Arrested at least once	47	15.2	136	10.4
Unknown	12	3.9	38	2.9
Total	309	100.0	1,302	100.0
After Beginning Drug Use				
Never arrested	112	36.2	192	14.7
Arrested at least once	138	44.7	936	71.9
No arrests, pre- or post-drug use	59	19.1	174	13.4
Total	309	100.0	1,302	100.0

Source: Compiled by the authors.

over 70 percent of the program clients had been arrested by the time of their entry into the county drug program, compared to 10 percent reporting arrests prior to initial drug use.

Finally, one would expect from the data presented thus far that fewer emergency-room patients than drug-program clients would have received prior treatment for drug problems. This prediction is supported by the data in Table 5.8. Over half of the program clients had been in treatment previously, compared to about 35 percent of the emergency-room patients.

TABLE 5.8

Prior Drug-Related Treatment Received by
Drug-Emergency Patients and
Drug-Program Clients

	Drug-Emergency Patients		Drug-Program Clients	
	Number	Percent	Number	Percent
No treatment experience	198	64.1	639	49.1
One or more treatment experiences	109	35.3	663	50.9
Unknown	2	.6	0	.0
Total	309	100.0	1,302	100.0

Source: Compiled by the authors.

SUMMARY

This brief chapter has reported quite a few differences between drug-emergency patients and drug-program clients. The largest of these differences, however, all bear directly on one thing: the nature of the drug involved in the patient/client's problem. Specifically, the majority of the drug-program clients are being treated for heroin problems, while almost half the drug-emergency patients were seen for a sedative or tranquilizer problem. The size of these differences is shown in Table 5.9, with other differences being reported in descending order, by size. The logical connection between the substance-type difference and the other reported differences between the populations is readily

TABLE 5.9

Summary of Major Differences between Drug-Emergency
Patients and Drug-Program Clients; Differences
of Under 15 Percent Reported in
Previous Eight Tables[a]

	Drug- Emergency Patients (N = 309)	Drug- Program Clients (N = 1,302)	Differences[b]
Heroin problem	16.2	58.1	-41.9
Sedative/tranquilizer problem	48.5	5.3	43.2
Obtained drug illegally	42.1	82.8	-40.7
Obtained drug legally	41.1	4.5	36.3
Arrested (post-drug use)	44.7	71.9	-27.2
Female	47.6	23.3	24.3
Male	52.4	76.0	-23.6
Black	26.5	50.5	-24.0
White	62.5	40.3	22.2
0-7 years of education	5.5	25.1	-19.6

First use of substance
  involved between
  ages 13 and 21
	42.7	61.4	-18.7

White-collar worker, housewife, or student	24.9	8.3	16.6
Treated previously	35.3	50.9	-15.6

[a]All sets of characteristics reported here have additional
categories; therefore, none of the sections of the table reports on
100.0 percent of the respondents in either population. See Tables
5.1 through 5.8.

[b]Negative difference indicates characteristic more prevalent
in program-client group; positive difference indicates characteristic
more prevalent in emergency-patient group.

Source: Compiled by the authors.

apparent, and becomes even more so when one recalls that most nonheroin substances involved in the drug-program admissions were other illegal drugs, and that many nonsedative/tranquilizer drugs involved in the drug-emergency cases were other legal drugs. Differences between the two populations in how drugs were obtained and contacts with official drug-user processing agencies are particularly easy to understand in this context.

But the characteristics of the two populations which are less directly connected to the type of drug involved are also important. Specifically, the emergency-room patients were clearly more likely to be female, white, and of white-collar status or a housewife or a student, while the drug-program clients were more likely to be male, black, without enough formal schooling to hold a decent job, and with a history of first drug use at an early age. These are the same basic demographic characteristics discussed in the previous chapter as differentiating sedative/tranquilizer-related from narcotics-related drug-emergency patients.

There would seem, then, to be two mutually interacting phenomena which represent the answer to the question posed at the beginning of this chapter. The question was: Why are so few drug-emergency patients referred to drug treatment programs and why do so few of them report prior treatment experience? The answers seem to be that (1) most of the Comprehensive Drug Program services are currently related to narcotics use, while most of the drug-emergency patients have a different kind of problem; and (2) the consequent differences between not only the drug problems but also—and perhaps more importantly—the social characteristics of the two populations in question make changes in the CDP programs difficult. That is, if it were primarily a young, black, lower-status male population which was becoming involved with sedatives and tranquilizers, adding this group to existing (illicit-drug) programs would be considerably easier in every respect. Potential clients would be less hesitant, existing clients would be more receptive, hospital personnel would have less reluctance to make program referrals, program personnel could make program adjustments more readily, and so forth. But, as we have seen, the growing population of persons involved with legal and licit substances is a rather different kind of group. It seems apparent, then, that Dade County drug-emergency cases will continue to be treated only as medical crises rather than as chances for drug-program referral until such time as deliberate changes are made in the treatment delivery network. (Chapter 7 discusses problems involved in attempting to make such changes.) The data presented in this chapter indicate that the change will have to be deliberate because the existing treatment system makes unplanned evolution of the programs unlikely to go in the needed direction.

6

ADVERSE ALCOHOL-REACTION PATIENTS
SEEN IN THE HOSPITAL EMERGENCY ROOM

The major focus of the Acute Drug Reactions Project was on
psychoactive drugs other than alcohol, particularly illicit substances
and prescription drugs. Beverage alcohol, however, is the most
widely used psychoactive substance in the United States. Over two-
thirds of the adult population use alcohol at least occasionally, and
over half drink once a month or more; further, alcohol is integrated
into many of our social customs and provides a food staple for many
people as well (see Chambers, Inciardi, and Siegal 1975; Cahalan,
Cisin, and Crossley 1969; NIAAA 1974). Of even greater consequence
for the subject of this study is the additional fact that alcohol is also
taken for its psychic effects. Drinking in order to deal with feelings
of anxiety, inadequacy, and depression is fairly common among
American drinkers; in a recent community study, for example,
Fallding and Miles (1974, p. 58) found that no less than 83 percent of
the drinkers in their sample acknowledged using drinking to make
difficult adjustments, particularly difficult social adjustments. This
means that alcohol is often used, as are other drugs, in a self-
medicating fashion to deal with difficult life situations. This mode
of use, plus the general prevalence of alcohol use in our society,
seemed to make alcohol an exceedingly appropriate additional topic
for the Acute Drug Reactions Project. Accordingly, data on adverse
alcohol reactions were included in several phases of the project.
Two of these phases--the referral followup experiment and the collection of drug-related death information--are discussed in the next
two chapters as more or less special subprojects of the main epidemiological study. Since both those chapters include data on alcohol
as well as other drugs, the present chapter provides some basic information on alcohol-reaction patients per se.

The first section of this chapter is a discussion of the nature
of adverse alcohol reactions, and is followed by a section describing
the procedures used in collecting the alcohol-related data in this
study. The next section parallels Chapter 2, in that it presents

baseline data on all alcohol-reaction cases seen at Jackson Memorial Hospital over a given period of time. Finally, detailed interview data from Miani and Denver--paralleling Chapter 4--are discussed at some length, with the emphasis being on the Jackson Memorial alcohol-emergency patients compared to those seen for adverse reactions to other drugs.

ADVERSE ALCOHOL REACTIONS

Adverse reactions to alcohol which are severe enough to bring a person to a hospital emergency room represent a fairly broad range of possible events. Many, but certainly not all, of these events are related in some way to alcoholism or "problem drinking" (generally defined as a drinking pattern involving the alcohol-related life problems but not necessarily the compulsiveness/loss of control typifying alcoholism). Current estimates (NIAAA 1974, p. 1) indicate that as many as ten million Americans can be classified as problem drinkers (including alcoholics). Numerous research studies have established that illness, accidents, and death from a wide variety of causes are all much more likely among heavy drinkers, and especially among alcoholics. This means that problem drinkers are involved in a disproportionate share of alcohol emergencies. However, it should be kept in mind during the following discussion that problem drinkers do not account for all alcohol emergencies, and in some cases they do not even represent the majority of emergency patients seen for particular alcohol-related problems.

Adverse reactions to alcohol can be categorized into three general types. The type in which an alcohol emergency is most directly related to alcohol itself involves conditions resulting from the physiological consequences of drinking. Major examples are acute hepatitis (a temporary liver inflammation caused by a toxic substance--in this case, more alcohol than the liver can deal with), severe withdrawal symptoms (most notably, delirium tremens), and a variety of conditions seen primarily in chronic alcoholics (such as alcoholic cirrhosis and Korsakoff's psychosis).

A second type of adverse reaction to alcohol is the kind of problem attributable to the indirect effect of alcohol on behavior, resulting in injuries being sustained. Most of these cases involve intoxication, although either the physical or the psychological concomitants of intoxication may be implicated in the particular injury. The psychological component is most evident, for example, in cases of attempted suicide or cases involving aggravated assault; studies indicate that both suicide and homicide, whether completed or unsuccessfully attempted, involve a high proportion of cases in which excessive alcohol use was implicated (Goodwin 1973; Mayfield and Montgomery 1972; Wolfgang and Strohm 1956). On the other hand, probably both psychological and physiological concomitants of intoxication are involved in alcohol-related injuries of the more obviously accidental type. For example, high blood alcohol concentrations have been estimated for between 15 percent and 33 percent of emergency-room patients appearing due to accidents at home or work, for 28-43 percent of fatally injured adult pedestrians, and for 40-55 percent of drivers involved in fatal motor vehicle crashes (Murray 1977, p. 97; NIAAA 1974, pp. 99-101). One other variety of adverse reactions to alcohol due to behavior while intoxicated is public intoxication. Prior to or as part of arrest procedures, persons given this designation by police officers are often brought to hospital emergency rooms.

Finally, a third route involves an adverse reaction occurring because of the combination of alcohol and some other psychoactive substance. It is well known that alcohol potentiates the effect of many other drugs. This implies that an adverse reaction would be less likely through the taking of the drug by itself or by drinking alone; when the two are ingested simultaneously--or in a problematic pattern--the potential for significant problems and/or difficulty is substantially heightened. The seriousness of this possibility is confirmed by recent data from the Drug Enforcement Administration's DAWN reports. Between July 1973 and April 1975, data from these reports (Project DAWN III, 1976) indicate that people presenting themselves for some sort of health service either in an emergency room or a crisis center with an alcohol-in-combination problem constituted about 8 percent of the acute drug reactions and the second most frequent drug category recorded by the DAWN system.

While these data indicate that alcohol in combination with other psychoactive substances is a significant problem, there exists little additional information about it. A number of epidemiological studies have suggested that alcohol abuse, especially that pattern we have labeled heavy drinking, is prevalent in our drug-using population; this extends to the use of both legal and illegal drugs. In terms of legal drug use or abuse, heavy drinkers constitute some 10 percent of the regular users of barbiturate drugs, some 15 percent of the users of minor tranquilizers, some 10 percent of the users of major tranquilizers, some 50 percent of the users of amphetamine pep pills and some 30 percent of the regular users of amphetamine diet pills (Chambers, Inciardi, and Siegal 1975). It should be repeated here that this heavy drinking in combination with barbiturates, hypnotics, and tranquilizers can present life-threatening situations because of the potentiating effect of alcohol. The possibility of an accidental overdose is significant in this group.

Looking at drug-use distributions from the opposite perspective--the percentage of heavy drinkers using other substances--we find that what little information exists is focused on alcoholics. This work does make it clear, however, that the use of sedatives and hypnotics by alcoholic persons is extensive (Freed 1973).

Research on street populations has also indicated that the use of alcohol in conjunction with other substances is quite prevalent in these groups. Skid row research in many cities has suggested that the use of diazepam and other tranquilizers by the skid row population is quite common; here, the vector of transmission typically involves medication received from legitimate medical sources (the VA is listed as a major source) and the use of these tranquilizers in conjunction with the usual range of alcoholic beverages. Another usage pattern is one in which methadone (maintenance) clients drink large quantities of wine in conjunction with their methadone; respondents report that the high obtained from this combination is an acceptable one. And Inciardi, Petersen, and Chambers (1974) have discussed the pattern of using wine in conjunction with methaqualone, a practice referred to in the street as the "lude-out."

All these observations argue that alcohol and other drugs are often used by the same people. The days in which drug users were seen as being separate from heavy or involved drinkers are past, and one would speculate they are unlikely to return. The pattern of polydrug use in which alcohol, the entirely legal and readily available substance, is providing the base for many other chemically induced states is now entirely commonplace.

In summary, prior studies have established that alcohol use can result in a rather varied assortment of medical emergencies and that such incidents occur to a considerable number of Americans. But a number of questions remain unanswered. One is the matter of how alcohol emergencies are distributed in general communities, as opposed to populations of alcoholics or other special drug-involved groups. Secondly, very few prior studies have been able to discuss alcohol-emergency patients and patients having adverse reactions to other drugs in the kind of direct comparison permitted by the data gathered in the Acute Drug Reactions Project. These two basic questions--distribution of alcohol emergencies in communities and comparison to drug emergencies--therefore constitute the main concerns of this chapter.

METHODOLOGY OF DATA COLLECTION

For purposes of the Acute Drug Reactions Project, an alcohol-related emergency was defined as one in which alcohol was the primary substance responsible for admission to the emergency room. The data collection procedures used for alcohol emergencies were precisely the same as the procedures used for other drug emergencies. Thus, for discussion of the instrument used in collecting data on all alcohol-emergency cases (Form A in the Appendix), see Chapter 2; similarly, the extended-interview instrument (Form B) and procedures used for the interview sample are discussed in Chapter 4. As was done for the drug emergencies, extended interviews were conducted in both Jackson Memorial Hospital, in Miami, and Denver General Hospital, in Denver. The sole difference between the alcohol and other drug data is that the baseline information on all substance-related admissions to Jackson Memorial was collected for the full five years of the project (1972-76) for the drug cases but for only the last 18 months (July 1975 through December 1976) for the alcohol cases.

Finally, it should be noted that much of the following analysis is presented in terms of alcohol versus drug cases, as if alcohol were not also a drug. This usage is employed solely for the sake of convenient terminology, since "drug" is an obviously briefer and hence more quickly understood term than "drugs other than alcohol."

SOCIAL AND DEMOGRAPHIC CHARACTERISTICS

Beginning in July 1975, the Acute Drug Reactions Project began collecting baseline data on acute alcohol reactions at the Jackson Memorial Hospital emergency room. For the period July 1, 1975 through December 31, 1976, a total of 5,004 emergency patients of this type were seen, and as suggested by Table 6.1, the majority were white or black males aged 35 years and above. The sex distribution is particularly striking. While the emergencies associated with other drugs were about equally likely to occur for males and females, alcohol emergencies were almost three times likelier among males than females. Table 6.2 reports the same kind of sex distribution among the Miami alcohol and drug patients who were interviewed as is seen in Table 6.1 for the total populations of emergency patients. Further, the distribution reported in Table 6.2 for the Denver alcohol patients shows even greater disparity between males and females, with the split being almost six males to one female (83 percent versus 17 percent).

These two tables also report fairly similar information on age. While the modal age category for drug patients was 18-24, it was the 35-49 category for alcohol patients. In fact, while only 20-25 percent of the drug-emergency patients were 35 years old or more, some 60-75 percent of the alcohol-emergency patients were that old

(60.4 percent of all Jackson Memorial's alcohol patients, 66.8 percent of those we were able to interview, and 74.6 percent of the Denver interview sample). Conversely, while 37-48 percent of the drug-emergency patients were 24 or younger, only about 8-13 percent of the alcohol-emergency patients fell into this category.

TABLE 6.1

Basic Demographic Characteristics of 5,004 Alcohol-
Emergency Patients and 4,054 Drug-Emergency
Patients, July 1, 1975-December 31, 1976

	All Alcohol Emergencies		All Drug Emergencies	
	Number	Percent	Number	Percent
Males	3,633	72.6	2,017	49.8
Females	1,368	27.3	2,034	50.2
No data	3	.1	3	<.1
Black	2,382	47.6	1,313	32.4
Hispanic	258	5.2	408	10.1
White	2,340	46.8	2,309	57.0
Other or no data	24	.5	24	.6
17 years and under	63	1.3	391	9.6
18-24 years	391	7.8	1,556	38.4
25-34 years	1,026	20.5	1,260	31.1
35-49 years	1,985	39.7	552	13.6
50 years and above	1,484	29.7	250	6.2
No data	55	1.1	45	1.1
Total	5,004	100.0	4,054	100.0

Source: Compiled by the authors.

The distribution by race and ethnicity, however, is not so simple to determine. The Denver interview samples for drug and alcohol patients (shown in Table 6.2) indicate a very high degree of similarity between them; 60 percent of both groups were white, 11-12 percent of both were black, and 19-21 percent were Mexican-American. The only large disparity is for American Indians, who were 2.1 percent of the Denver drug-emergency patients interviewed but 4.4 percent of the alcohol sample; these are such small percentages, however, that caution in their interpretation seems advisable.

The Miami race and ethnicity distributions look somewhat different. Table 6.1 indicates that blacks and whites represented a very similar number of all Jackson Memorial's alcohol-emergency cases (about 47 percent in each case), while Hispanics accounted for only about 5 percent of them. Recalling that the Dade County population is approximately 61 percent white, 24 percent Hispanic, and 15 percent black, Hispanics are obviously greatly underrepresented in the alcohol emergencies (even more so than in the drug emergencies), and blacks are greatly overrepresented (again, even more so than in the drug emergencies). That is:

	White	Hispanic	Black
Dade County	61%	24%	15%
Drug emergencies	57	10	32
Alcohol emergencies	47	5	48

This distribution for alcohol emergencies, it might be noted, is approximately the same as that for the Miami narcotics cases discussed in Chapter 4 (see Table 4.18), as is the sex distribution of the alcohol patients (but not the age distribution, since the narcotics patients tended to be considerably younger than the alcohol patients).

A curious problem arises, however, if one compares the Miami alcohol population shown in Table 6.1 with the Miami alcohol interview sample in Table 6.2. The two are very similar in sex and age distributions, but not in race and ethnicity (whereas the drug-emergency population and sample had matched up fairly well on all three characteristics; see Chapter 4). Specifically, whites represented 46.8 percent of all alcohol-emergency patients seen at Jackson Memorial during this period, but were 69.6 percent of the alcohol-emergency patients interviewed; blacks, conversely, were 47.6 percent of the alcohol population, but only 25.3 percent of those interviewed. The other, smaller differences between the population and sample can be explained, it will be recalled, on the basis of the tendency of the interviewing procedures to select the more serious cases. Reasons do exist for thinking that the same explanation may hold for the sample-population disparity on race as well as for that on age and sex--that is, for thinking that the white alcohol-emergency patients tend to have more serious problems. However, consideration of these reasons requires sufficiently detailed examination of the data so that this discussion will be given in a later section of the chapter.

To summarise these data, the bulk of the alcohol-emergency interview data (which is the basis for all the rest of the discussion of social characteristics of the alcohol patients), from both Miami and Denver, indicates that we are looking at an older, male, and primarily white population. What this implies is that many of these patients may be classified as skid row drinkers or homeless alcoholics.

TABLE 6.2

Basic Demographic Characteristics of Alcohol-Emergency
Patients Interviewed in Two Cities, Compared to Drug-
Emergency Patients Interviewed during the Same Period

| | Miami Interviews | | Denver Interviews | |
	Alcohol	Drugs	Alcohol	Drugs
Male	75.1%	52.4%	82.8%	44.2%
Female	24.9	47.6	17.2	55.8
White	69.6	62.5	60.0	60.2
Black	25.3	26.5	10.7	12.0
American Indian	.0	.6	4.4	2.1
Mexican-American	.5	.0	18.8	20.9
Cuban/Hispanic	3.3	9.3	5.8	3.8
Other	.0	.6	.2	1.1
Unknown	1.4	.3	.0	.0
17 years and under	1.4	3.2	.6	3.8
18-24 years	11.1	38.2	6.9	33.5
25-34 years	18.0	37.9	17.8	38.5
35-49 years	38.7	13.6	44.4	16.4
50 years and above	28.1	7.1	30.2	7.8
Unknown	2.8	.0	.0	.4
Total	217	309	478	527

Source: Compiled by the authors.

This idea is given some support in a comparison of the marital status of the Miami alcohol patients versus that of the Miami drug patients, since this kind of data reveals both marital status and some indication about current living arrangement. The results were in keeping with our expectations about some of the differences separating the two populations. For one thing, a larger percentage of the drug patients report never being married (43.4 percent versus 23.5 percent). This probably reflects a number of trends: that the drug population is probably younger than the alcohol population; and that the alcohol population is likely to be somewhat more traditional in outlook, especially in the values concerning marriage and family (which is not to say they are necessarily capable of sustaining this kind of ongoing relationship, however). When we consider the categories of those that are married and those in common-law marriage, the two groups look more similar. Here, 21.7 percent of the drug patients and 18.4 percent of the alcohol patients report involvement in such an arrangement.

The category that indicates people were married but are now either separated or divorced provides the most significant data. Within the drug group, a third (33.3 percent) of the sample reports being separated or divorced. But in the alcohol sample, fully half of the respondents (50.3 percent) are either separated or divorced. A small proportion of each group also reports being widowed--1.6 percent of the drug patients and 7.8 percent of the alcohol patients. This figure is understandably higher among the alcohol group, since they are significantly older than the drug group.

The implications of these data are clear. They indicate that the alcohol patients are essentially a socially isolated group, with over 80 percent of this population reporting that they are "alone in the world"; unmarried, widowed, separated or divorced, these people are socially isolated. This implies that the alcohol population might be characterized as a rootless, ungrounded group.

This implication is further supported when we examine the current living arrangements of the same group. Some 42 percent of the Miami alcohol patients reported living entirely alone. An additional 14 percent were living with a spouse (either legal or common law). The remainder of the respondents reported living with parents, relations, or others. It should be noted, however, that some 17 percent said they were living with "a friend or friends." Often this constitutes a somewhat unstable relationship and points once again to the essential rootlessness of this population.

We see some of the possible reasons for this in the data on educational achievement reported in Table 6.3. Among the Miami alcohol patients, the majority have little education: some 55 percent have no high-school diploma and only about 12 percent have any training beyond high school. Similar observations might be made about the Miami drug patients, but about 10 percent more of these people had at least graduated from high school. Thus, the Miami alcohol-emergency patients have generally completed even less formal education than their drug-emergency counterparts, even though they tend to be a considerably older group. Table 6.3 also indicates, however, that relatively little difference exists between the Denver alcohol- and drug-emergency patients in respect to education; the figures for both groups bear a strong resemblance to those for the Miami drug patients.

TABLE 6.3

Educational Attainment and Usual Occupation of Alcohol- and
Drug-Emergency Patients Interviewed in Two Cities

	Miami Interviews		Denver Interviews	
	Alcohol	Drugs	Alcohol	Drugs
0-7 years	11.5%	5.5%	9.0%	6.3%
8-11 years	43.3	38.2	38.8	40.2
High school diploma	28.1	37.5	37.0	40.8
Post-high school/vocational	4.6	6.1	8.8	5.5
Junior college degree				
or more	7.4	5.8	6.3	6.3
Unknown	5.1	6.8	.2	.5
PTMA[a]	9.2	9.3	11.7	11.0
Sales, clerical	7.8	19.8	8.7	12.9
Skilled, semi-skilled	30.4	20.7	33.5	18.6
Unskilled, service[b]	42.4	34.7	40.4	43.4
Not in labor force[c]	6.9	9.4	5.3	11.4
Unknown	3.2	6.1	.4	2.7
Total	217	309	478	527

[a]Professional-technical and management-administrative.
[b]Including "usually unemployed" responses.
[c]Housewife, student, other.
Source: Compiled by the authors.

Data on occupation, then, is as one might expect, given the
education information. In Miami, slightly more of the alcohol than
drug patients reported being unemployed at the time of the emergency-
room interview (65 percent versus 57 percent)--with the difference
being roughly the same size as the difference between them in regard
to having graduated from high school. Similarly, about 12 percent
more of the drug than alcohol patients in Miami reported white-
collar positions as their usual occupation, while some 19 percent
more of the alcohol patients reported a usually blue-collar occupation (see Table 6.3). Again, however, the two groups are more
similar in Denver. The only large differences were that more of
the alcohol patients usually held skilled or semiskilled jobs (33.5
percent versus 18.6 percent for the drug patients), and that the drug
patients were about twice as likely to not usually be in the labor force

(11.4 percent versus 5.3 percent); the latter difference reflects both the age and sex disparities between the drug and alcohol patients, since the not-usually-in-the-labor-force category consists primarily of students and housewives.

Finally, the four samples were also compared on public assistance history, but differences between the drug and alcohol samples on this factor were generally very small. The only noteworthy difference concerned the question of whether an individual had ever received public monies. In both cities, about 51 percent of the drug patients reported never having received public assistance, compared to 44 percent of the alcohol patients. Again, however, this difference is doubtless a reflection of the age disparities between the drug and alcohol patients. Older persons obviously have a longer period during which they could have received some kind of assistance, and they are also likelier to be eligible for certain kinds of payments, such as Social Security of Veterans Administration benefits.

In summarizing the general social and demographic characteristics of the alcohol-emergency patients, then, one can say that they are primarily older males, and are likely to be either white or black, but are more likely to be black than one would expect from general population distributions; they are generally of low educational- and occupational-status levels, and have a high rate of both unemployment and recourse to public assistance. The primary differences between them and patients seen for adverse reactions to other drugs are that the alcohol patients are considerably likelier to be male and over 35 and somewhat likelier to be minority group members, in a usually blue-collar rather than white-collar occupation, and without a high school education or present employment.

REASON FOR COMING TO THE HOSPITAL

The alcohol patients sought emergency treatment at Jackson Memorial Hospital for much the same reasons as drug patients did, but in a different proportional distribution. As indicated in Table 6.4, accidental overdoses, psychotic/panic reactions, alcoholism (undifferentiated), and cirrhosis accounted for almost two-thirds of the complaints. The vast majority of these individuals were conscious at the time of admission (94.2 percent), a very comparable situation to that indicated in Table 2.5 for drug-emergency patients. A further dissimilarity between the populations, however, is indicated by the fact that only 1.6 percent (N = 78) of the alcohol patients reported an emergency problem with some secondary substance (usually a depressant or marijuana). Almost half the patients with adverse reactions to other drugs, by contrast, reported the involvement of secondary substances; further, the most commonly reported secondary substance was alcohol (indicated by about 19 percent of all drug patients interviewed at Jackson Memorial; see Table 4.8).

TABLE 6.4

Complaint at Admission of All Jackson Memorial Hospital
Alcohol-Emergency Patients, July 1, 1975-December 31, 1976

	Number	Percent
Attempted suicide	18	3.6
Accidental overdose	856	17.1
Allergic reactions	3	.1
Addiction problems	440	8.8
Infections	105	2.1
Psychotic/panic reactions	978	19.6
Public intoxication	429	8.6
Alcoholism (undifferentiated)	543	10.9
Delirium tremens	197	3.9
Cirrhosis	874	17.5
All other	555	11.1
No data	6	.1
Total	5,004	100.0

Source: Compiled by the authors.

Further data on where alcohol-emergency patients ended up at Jackson Memorial is provided in Table 6.5. This compares the Miami drug and alcohol interview samples in regard to the emergency unit at which the respondents were initially admitted. These data seem to indicate that people suffering from an acute drug reaction are more likely to seek service in a hospital unit offering medical services. The difference is observed at some 12 percentage points. It is likely that this reflects the more medical-emergency nature of a drug problem such as a state of unconsciousness or respiratory difficulties; in this situation the presentation for medical treatment is entirely appropriate. The figures for psychiatric emergencies, on the other hand, appear to be very similar for the drug and alcohol samples; these emergencies would entail disorientation, agitation, and confusion as the presenting symptoms. But a significant difference appears in regard to presentation in the jail ward of the hospital. Some 41 percent of the alcohol-emergency patients were admitted in the jail ward, compared to 27 percent of the drug sample. This obviously reflects differences in law enforcement procedures, but it is also affected by differences between drug types and drug-user types. For example, if police discover a comatose individual who appears to be drunk, or a skid row resident in distress, they are likely to take him to the jail unit of the hospital rather than put him into a city lockup. In the case of drugs, however, it is probably somewhat more difficult to make the presumption that a drug overduse is responsible for the individual's condition. In addition, severely intoxicated persons who are arrested while operating a motor vehicle may be taken to the jail unit for medical tests to determine their level of intoxication; again, this is more likely to take place with alcohol than other drugs.

TABLE 6.5

Initial Hospital Emergency Unit Admitting Alcohol- and Drug-Emergency Patients Interviewed at Jackson Memorial

| | Alcohol Patients | | Drug Patients | |
	Number	Percent	Number	Percent
Medical	47	21.7	104	33.7
Psychiatric	81	37.3	121	39.2
Jail	89	41.0	82	26.5
Unknown	0	.0	2	.6
Total	217	100.0	309	100.0

Source: Compiled by the authors.

GENERAL DRUG-USE PATTERNS

Strongly related to the matter of how and why individuals end up at an emergency room for an alcohol-related problem is, of course, the question of their general drug-use patterns, particularly in regard to alcohol.

Estimating typical alcohol consumption, however, is somewhat more involved than the measurement of other drug use. One major reason for this is that alcohol use is so much a part of our culture and alcohol is used in so many different ways that people typically give little thought to their drinking. It therefore becomes difficult to derive meaningful data from a simple yes-no dichotomy of drinking. People drink in different frequencies, drink different amounts, and tend to vary their drinking patterns. What is therefore needed is an index incorporating measures of several factors: the quantity, the frequency, and the consistency (or variability) of an individual's alcohol consumption. These three considerations are in fact all taken into account by a drinking classification called a Q-F-V index (for quantity-frequency-variability; see Cahalan, Cisin, and Crossley 1969, for index-construction details). This index classifies individuals into five groups, each representing a particular drinking pattern. These groups are:

1. Abstainers--those persons who drink alcoholic beverages less than once a year, or never.
2. Infrequent drinkers--persons who drink at least once a year but less than once a month.
3. Light drinkers--persons who generally limit their alcoholic intake to one or two drinks, or who drink a bit more than this but only drink once or twice a month.
4. Moderate drinkers--persons who characteristically drink several times during a week but almost always limit their consumption to three or four drinks on each occasion or, again, who usually have a few more drinks than this, but drink only once or twice a month.
5. Heavy drinkers--persons who typically drink every day and for whom it is not unusual to consume five or six drinks on each occasion, or fewer drinks per sitting but several times a day, or less often but almost invariably five or more drinks.

This index has been used in numerous state- and national-level surveys of drinking practices. While an individual's classification will not indicate exactly how much he drinks or his exact level of intoxication, what it does do is differentiate between general types of drinking with considerably more meaningfulness than a simple yes-no dichotomy or information on only one of the three dimensions encompassed in the index.

When we used the Q-F-V index with the alcohol-emergency patients, we found that almost all of them--85 percent of the Miami patients and 94 percent of those in Denver--fell into the heavy-drinker category. This is in dramatic contrast to general household-population surveys, which find about 12 percent of all adult Americans to be in this category. It is even a considerably higher percentage of heavy drinkers than we found among the drug-emergency patients interviewed: 42 percent in Miami, and 52 percent in Denver.

Looking at the Q-F-V results in more detail, consider the contrast between the Miami alcohol-emergency sample and the random household-population sample reported on by Cahalan, Cisin, and Crossley (1969, pp. 18-20):

	U.S. Adult Population	Miami Alcohol Patients
Abstainers	32%	5%
Infrequent drinkers	15	3
Light drinkers	28	4
Moderate drinkers	13	4
Heavy drinkers	12	83

These data leave little room for multiple interpretations: such a great majority of the alcohol-emergency patients can be classified as heavy drinkers that there is a high probability of a good many of them being alcohol abusers or problem drinkers. Because of the overwhelming representation of heavy drinkers, further references to drinking classifications in this study are broken down into heavy drinkers and "all others."

We should perhaps first speak, however, to the question of abstainers among the alcohol patients. Ten people in the Miami alcohol sample were listed as abstainers (constituting 4.7 percent of the sample). Inasmuch as they were people admitted to an emergency room for some sort of alcohol-related crisis, these findings are difficult to explain. The only logical conclusion is that at least most of these respondents were not accurately representing their drinking patterns when questions were asked. This is not entirely surprising when we consider that underreporting of frequency or quantity of alcohol consumption has long been recognized as a major problem for alcohol researchers.

When the Q-F-V distinction between heavy drinkers and lighter-drinking classifications was cross-tabulated by the major social and demographic characteristics for the Miami sample, nothing very surprising was revealed. As Table 6.6 indicates, heavy drinking was more prevalent among patients who were male, over 25, or unemployed. It was also more likely among persons with either less or more than a high school education; this is interesting, but our data permit little elucidation of the reason for it. It might be noted, however, that eight of the ten abstainers were located in the high-school-diploma-only category. Perhaps less-educated people are likelier to see themselves as members of a street population of some sort, and hence are more willing to admit heavy alcohol use; similarly, perhaps those with more education are also more willing to report their drinking patterns accurately because they attach less moral or emotional significance to drinking than the high school educated.

TABLE 6.6

Heavy Drinking versus Other Drinking Classifications among
Selected Social and Demographic Subgroups of the Alcohol-
Emergency Patients Interviewed in Miami[a]

	(N)	Heavy (percent)	Other (percent)
Male	(163)	86.5	13.5
Female	(54)	79.6	20.4
Black	(55)	83.6	16.4
Hispanic	(8)	100.0	0.0
White	(151)	84.1	15.9
Under 25	(28)	67.9	32.1
25-34 years	(39)	87.2	12.8
35-49 years	(85)	88.2	11.8
50 years and above	(62)	85.5	14.5
Less than high school	(117)	88.0	12.0
High school diploma[b]	(61)	70.5	29.5
More	(26)	96.2	0.0
Employed	(77)	79.2	19.5
Unemployed	(140)	87.9	12.1
Total sample	(217)	83.4	15.2

[a]Where percentages do not add across to 100.0 percent of the
N, the remainder is due to missing data on the subgroup characteristic or drinking classification or both.

[b]Including GED (high school equivalency diploma).

Source: Compiled by the authors.

Turning to the subject of drugs other than alcohol, we found
that having at least tried other substances was not uncommon among
the alcohol patients (see Table 6.7). Four classes of drugs can be
identified as having been used by a fair number of the Miami sample:
(1) barbiturates, (2) other sedatives and hypnotics, (3) minor tranquilizers, and (4) marijuana/hashish. The use of barbiturates and
other sedatives and hypnotics by alcohol-abusing people is not unusual. The effects of these drugs are similar in many ways to those
of alcohol. Moreover, many of the tranquilizers, especially diazepam

(Valium), are supplied in substantial quantities by various treatment centers and private physicians. Table 6.7 indicates that the alcohol patients represent a drug-experimenting group, although they are not nearly as much of one as was the Miami drug-patient sample. The percentages of alcohol patients reporting having ever used the various drug types are consistently close to only half those for the drug patients. The exceptions are drugs with too little current use among alcohol patients to even merit entry in the table: heroin, methadone, other narcotics, cocaine, and LSD--for which the alcohol patients' percentages on having ever used are only a third to a fourth those of the drug patients (see Table 4.11 for the drug-patient data).

TABLE 6.7

Drug-Use Experience of Alcohol- and Drug-Emergency
Patients Interviewed in Miami: Percentage Reporting
Any and Current Use of Selected Substances[a]

	Ever Used		Current Use	
	Alcohol Sample (N = 217)	Drug Sample (N = 309)	Alcohol Sample (N = 217)	Drug Sample (N = 309)
Marijuana	34.1	65.0	19.4	50.1
Minor tranquilizers	35.4	58.6	16.1	35.9
Major tranquilizers	12.9	27.8	9.2	12.0
Barbiturates	24.8	52.4	7.4	27.8
Other sedatives	22.1	48.2	6.9	27.2
Analgesics[b]	16.5	25.9	6.9	12.0
Antidepressants	9.2	18.8	5.1	6.1
Alcohol			95.4	74.1

[a]In order of frequency of current use by the alcohol-emergency patients (except for alcohol). Note: due to multiple responses, percentages do not add to 100 percent.
[b]Nonnarcotic analgesics.
Source: Compiled by the authors.

Current use of other drugs is even more disparate, with, for example, only about 7 percent of the alcohol patients reporting current use of barbiturates or of other sedatives--figures which are 20 percent less than those for the drug-reaction patients. Only two substances other than alcohol were reported as currently used by more than 9 percent of the alcohol patients: marijuana (19 percent) and minor tranquilizers (16 percent). These figures seem to indicate two things about the drug-use patterns of the alcohol-reaction patients. First, the "ever used" reports from them are high enough to indicate that, at least at some point in their lives, many of them were drug experimenters. But, second, the current-use figures indicate that the great majority of the alcohol-reaction patients had, by the time of their appearance at the emergency room, focused rather completely on alcohol use. This again raises the possibility that the alcohol-emergency sample was largely a skid row group.

In part with the idea of identifying such a group, another interview question was asked about the consumption of nonbeverage alcohol. This includes substances such as Sterno (canned fuel), paint thinner, rubbing alcohol, and shaving lotion. Prevalent use of such materials indicates that a population might be considered a homeless or skid row one. The data indicate that some 14 percent of the alcohol patients had tried a nonbeverage alcohol. Approximately half of these, some 7 percent or 14 respondents, indicated they currently drink some nonbeverage alcohol. Needless to say, the steady use of these chemicals can only force the individual into some kind of medical crisis.

When we consider the race and sex of the nonbeverage-alcohol users the data further confirm the skid row assumption. Non-beverage-alcohol use is almost exclusively a white and male phenomenon, and these are the groups which constitute the largest part of the skid row-type population. Specifically, of 14 current non-beverage-alcohol users, all were male and 13 were white; of 15 former users, 13 were male and 12 were white. In addition there is also some indication of a positive association between nonbeverage-alcohol use and age, with the older cohorts the principal consumers.

At this point in the chapter it seems appropriate to return to the question left unanswered in our discussion of race: why were whites so overrepresented among the alcohol patients interviewed? While whites were 47 percent of Jackson Memorial's alcohol-emergency patients during this period, they were almost 70 percent of our alcohol sample. As noted previously, other biases in the interview procedures--toward somewhat older patients and toward more life-threatening drugs--were apparently a bias toward overselection of the more serious cases; the more serious the case, the longer the patient would be around the emergency room, and hence the better the chance of an interview taking place. But why would whites with alcohol emergencies tend to be more serious cases than blacks?

Part of the answer is provided in the data on nonbeverage alcohol just discussed. While whites were 47 percent of the alcohol patients, and 70 percent of the alcohol sample, they accounted for 90 percent of the 29 patients admitting having previously used nonbeverage alcohol and 92 percent of the 14 patients admitting current nonbeverage-alcohol use. Since this kind of substance is considerably more toxic than beverage alcohol, its most typical users--whites--run a greater risk of having a serious medical emergency.

Given these differences, one begins to wonder about other drug-use differences between white and black alcohol-emergency patients. We looked at Q-F-V scores, but found that 84 percent of both black and white patients were classified as heavy drinkers (see Table 6.6). But for use of prescription drugs--drugs which might interact with alcohol and hence precipitate a medical emergency, especially for a heavy drinker--we found racial differences almost as large as those for nonbeverage alcohol. As Table 6.8 indicates, while whites represented 70 percent of the alcohol-emergency sample, they accounted for 86-87 percent of the minor-tranquilizer, analgesic, and nonbarbiturate sedative users among these patients, 90 percent of the major-tranquilizers users, and 94 percent of the barbiturate users. Given the potentially lethal effects of combining alcohol with any of these drugs, it is not surprising to find that the subgroup more likely to use both (whites) appeared more frequently in a sample biased toward more serious cases.

TABLE 6.8

Use of Substances Other than Beverage Alcohol among Alcohol-Emergency Patients Interviewed in Miami, by Race*

	Whites	Blacks	N
Nonbeverage-alcohol users	92.9	7.1	14
Minor tranquilizer users	85.7	11.4	35
Major tranquilizer users	90.0	5.0	20
Barbiturate users	93.8	6.3	16
Other sedative users	86.6	6.7	15
Analgesic users	86.6	13.3	15
Antidepressant users	81.8	18.2	11
Alcohol-emergency sample	69.6	25.3	217

*All rows of figures do not add across to 100.0 percent as Hispanic cases are not presented here due to the small number of Hispanics involved in alcohol emergencies at Jackson Memorial Hospital (only 5.2 percent of all cases during the period, while being about 24 percent of the Dade County population).

Source: Compiled by the authors.

In short, while the alcohol interviews did not result in a description of the entire alcohol-reactions population, these data indicate that our sample probably does provide a rather adequate description of the actual population of serious alcohol-reaction cases.

PRIOR CONTACT WITH COMMUNITY AGENCIES

Earlier in the study it was emphasized that treatment for substance-abuse problems was not nearly as common among drug-emergency patients as one would expect, given the drug-use experience of these people. We found a similar situation with the alcohol-emergency patients. While about 35 percent of the Miami drug patients interviewed reported participation in a drug treatment program, some 37 percent (N = 80) of the alcohol patients interviewed in Miami indicated they had received some treatment for alcohol-related problems, and an additional eight respondents (3.7 percent) reported being currently in treatment for alcohol-related problems. Table 6.9 reports the type of alcohol-related treatment received by these patients, and also indicates that the Miami patients were considerably less likely to have received treatment of any kind than were the alcohol patients interviewed in Denver. The majority of the Denver sample, some 55 percent, reported either being in treatment or having had treatment in the past; 24 percent of the Denver sample reported being in treatment currently. This raises a number of questions which cannot be resolved here, most notably questions about the efficacy of the treatment that the Denver patients had received.

We also looked at number of prior treatment experiences. We found that of those people in the Miami sample who had undergone treatment for alcohol-related problems, 42 percent had been treated in one program, 20 percent reported that they had been involved in two programs, and 13 percent in three programs. Fourteen percent of this population report obtaining treatment in seven or more programs. One must necessarily conclude from these data that the alcohol-emergency patients included a subpopulation which has had much experience with the service delivery network for alcohol-related problems. Again, the fact that a significant number of people report being in treatment for alcohol-related problems and yet are again presenting themselves with an alcohol-related emergency/crisis raises some serious questions about the nature of the services delivered.

A few of these questions are approached, it might be noted, in the breakdown of the kinds of treatment received by alcohol-emergency patients, reported in Table 6.9 for both Miami and

Denver. In both cities inpatient detoxification (likely to be three days) is the most common form of treatment experience. Some 28 percent of the Miami sample and 84 percent of the Denver sample report having had this kind of treatment service. Inpatient detoxification, however, is more accurately considered an extended form of alcohol-emergency medical treatment than a form (however brief) of treatment for alcohol abuse. When experience in programs having a social/psychological--as opposed to chemical--orientation is considered, relatively small percentages of these patients were found to have received treatment. For example, only 11 percent in Miami and 12 percent in Denver report treatment provided by a community mental health center of one sort of another, including Alcoholics Anonymous. Similarly, only 8 percent in Miami and 13 percent in Denver had exposure to a residential treatment program.

TABLE 6.9

Type of Prior Alcohol Treatment Received by Alcohol-
Emergency Patients Interviewed in Two Cities

	Miami Alcohol Patients (N = 217)	Denver Alcohol Patients (N = 478)
Residential	7.8%	13.2%
Antagonist	2.3	41.6
Public inpatient	4.6	16.3
Private inpatient	1.8	3.8
Outpatient department	1.8	1.5
Inpatient detoxification	28.1	83.5
Other inpatient	1.4	7.5
Community mental health center	10.6	12.3
Day care	.9	.4
Private therapy	.9	1.5
Other	3.2	13.2

*Percentages do not add to 100 percent due to multiple treatment episodes.
Source: Compiled by the authors.

Why had the majority of the alcohol patients we interviewed received no prior treatment for alcohol problems? Part of the answer may be reflected in the disposition data we recorded for all alcohol-emergency patients during this period at Jackson Memorial

Hospital. As Table 6.10 indicates, more patients were treated and released (34.1) than were treated and referred to other agencies (28.7 percent).

TABLE 6.10

Disposition of All Jackson Memorial Hospital Alcohol-Emergency Patients, July 1, 1975–December 31, 1976

	Number	Percent
Left without treatment	96	1.9
Treated and released	1,706	34.1
Treated, left against medical advice	126	2.5
Treated and referred	1,437	28.7
Admitted to psychiatry	221	4.4
Admitted to medical unit	612	12.2
Transferred to jail	764	15.3
No data	42	.8
Total	5,004	100.0

Source: Compiled by the authors.

Of the 1,437 patients referred, almost half were referrals to the Dade County Comprehensive Alcohol Program, and about 17 percent were to the hospital's crisis intervention center (see Table 6.11). These figures indicate that about the same proportion of Jackson Memorial alcohol patients as drug patients were referred to other agencies, but that alcohol patients were somewhat more likely to be referred to an alcohol or drug program than were the drug patients. Still, as Table 6.10 implies, under 14 percent of all Miami patients seen for alcohol emergencies were referred to the Dade County Comprehensive Alcohol Program. Both drug and alcohol patients, then, were referred to treatment programs less often than might be expected and, accordingly, the majority of both groups had no prior treatment experience.

But although the alcohol- and drug-emergency patients were fairly similar in terms of prior contact with treatment agencies, they were rather different in prior contacts with the criminal justice system. Table 6.12 reports the arrest history of the alcohol and drug samples in Miami and Denver. In Miami two-thirds of the drug sample had been arrested, and in Denver more than half of the drug sample had been arrested. As high as these figures are, when the alcohol population is considered, an even more impressive arrest history is observed. In Miami, some 84 percent of the alcohol respondents reported having been arrested, as did a highly similar 81 percent of the Denver alcohol respondents. This is entirely in keeping with what we know about the behavior of alcohol-troubled persons. Involvement with the law is very common, most typically through such offenses as being drunk and disorderly, public intoxication, and driving while under the influence of alcohol. In fact, repeated contact with the criminal justice system is one of the hallmarks of the homeless alcoholic.

TABLE 6.11

Community Service Agency Referrals among All Jackson Memorial Hospital Alcohol-Emergency Patients, July 1, 1975-December 31, 1976

	Number	Percent
Comprehensive alcohol program	685	13.7
Comprehensive drug program	27	.5
Crisis intervention clinic	249	5.0
Outpatient department	8	.2
Other hospital	96	1.9
Private psychiatrist	13	.3
JMH detoxification	36	.7
Welfare	63	1.3
Other agencies	192	3.8
No referral	3,567	71.3
No data	68	1.3
Total	5,004	100.0

Source: Compiled by the authors.

Further, the drug and alcohol samples were different in that the alcohol patients tended to have their first arrest at a later age. In the Miami samples, for example, about 54 percent of the drug patients had their first arrest before the age of 25, compared to 44 percent of the alcohol patients. Interestingly, within the next ten-year period, that is, between ages 25 and 34, the alcohol and drug curves equalize. In both cases some 60 percent of the population had their first arrest before the age of 35. This suggests that the drug population was probably more visible at an earlier age. Alcohol-troubled people tend to maintain their social position for a longer period of time than heavy users of other drugs. This implies that there are social processes buffering the alcohol-troubled person from problems with law enforcement agencies, and, more significantly, that by the time a law enforcement agency does become aware of the individual's problem, his behavior has deteriorated significantly.

TABLE 6.12

Arrest History of Alcohol- and Drug-Emergency
Patients Interviewed in Two Cities

	Miami Interviews		Denver Interviews	
	Alcohol	Drug	Alcohol	Drug
	(percent)		(percent)	
Arrested	83.9	66.7	81.2	51.6
Never arrested	15.7	32.7	18.8	47.8
No data	.5	.6	.0	.6
Total number	217	309	478	527

Source: Compiled by the authors.

In fact, overall arrest reports indicate that the alcohol patients had more trouble with the law than the drug patients. For example, some 49 percent of the Miami alcohol sample reported being arrested during the previous two years, compared to 38 percent of the Miami drug sample.

Similarly, and still using data from Miami, among the drug sample some 33 percent reported no history of arrest, but among the alcohol sample only about 16 percent reported no history of arrest. Returning to the other end of the scale, multiple arrests (here meaning in excess of 20 incidents) account for only 4.5 percent of the Miami drug group while accounting for 13.4 percent of the alcohol cohort. In terms of aggregates, the mean number of arrests in the drug sample is 5.6 whereas the mean number of arrests in the alcohol population is 7.7. Clearly, the alcohol population has had a more extensive involvement with the criminal justice system.

When the nature of the criminal involvement is considered, further differences emerge between the Miami drug and alcohol patients. Higher proportions of the alcohol sample report never having been involved in property crimes (68 percent versus 56 percent), although the percentages in the two samples reporting crimes against persons are very similar (and quite low). But substance abuse per se is even more likely to represent the typical crime the alcohol patient was involved in than is the case for the drug patients. These victimless crimes for the alcohol abuser usually involve public intoxication or some similar offense, such as vagrancy--for which a nonalcohol-substance abuser is less likely to be charged.

Finally, we also examined the relationship between arrest history and heavy drinking. It must be remembered, of course, that whether the two are causally related or simply tied into the same lifestyle, or both, is not revealed by the data. We do know, however, that almost a third of the Miami alcohol sample was brought to Jackson Memorial because of public intoxication. If they were brought in by police officers, an arrest is obviously likely to have accompanied heavy drinking of this type. Table 6.13 indicates that some 86 percent of the heavy drinkers in the Miami alcohol sample have been arrested at one time or another, compared to 73 percent of the other patients in the sample. Very similar percentages appear for the Denver alcohol sample. The difference between the arrest history of heavy drinkers and of those in all other drinking classifications for the two drug samples is also shown in Table 6.13. In Miami, the difference is again small, with only about 10 percent more of the heavy drinkers having been arrested; in Denver, however, there is a difference of about 20 percent. Overall, these figures do seem to indicate that although it is probably not a strong relationship, there generally is some degree of association between heavy drinking and being arrested among these patients; this is indicated by the fact that in all four samples, heavy drinkers were more likely than others to report they had previously been arrested.

To summarize, although not identical, prior contacts with community agencies were in many ways similar among the drug and alcohol samples. A limited number of the patients in each group had been in a treatment program (about a third of each), but relatively few people were in a treatment program at the time of the emergency-room episode. Prior contacts with police and courts were more frequent. For both drug and alcohol patients, more persons had been arrested, arrested within the last two years, and even convicted than had ever been enrolled in a treatment program. The fact that some 80 percent of the alcohol patients had been arrested at least once, combined with information from previous sections of this chapter, again suggests that the bulk of the alcohol-reaction sample appears to represent a skid row population: older, socially isolated, low-status white males whose lives are heavily involved with drinking and the "revolving door" of the criminal justice system (Pittman and Gordon 1958).

TABLE 6.13

Arrest History of Alcohol- and Drug-Emergency Patients Interviewed in Two Cities, by Drinking Classification: Percentage of Heavy Drinkers and of All Other Patients Who Had Been Arrested[a]

	Heavy Drinkers		All Others		(No Data)[b]
	Arrested	Total	Arrested	Total	
Miami samples					
Alcohol (N = 217)	86.3%	183	72.7%	33	(1)
Drug (N = 309)	73.4	128	62.6	179	(2)
Denver samples					
Alcohol (N = 478)	81.6	451	74.1	27	(0)
Drug (N = 527)	61.8	272	41.3	252	(3)

[a]As an example of how to read this table, note the first line: Of the 183 heavy drinkers in the Miami alcohol sample, 86.3 percent had been arrested--compared to 72.7 percent of the 33 other patients in the sample; 183 heavy drinkers plus 33 others plus 1 case with missing data totals 217, the total patients in the sample.

[b]Data missing on drinking classification or arrest history or both.

Source: Compiled by the authors.

Further, first arrests for alcohol patients tended to take place when the patients were rather young, but not as young as in the case of the drug patients. Finally, for both alcohol and drug patients, drug crimes were the most frequently reported type of crime committed, followed--not very closely, in the case of the alcohol sample--by property crimes and, at considerably lower rates, personal crimes. The major difference between the samples was that the alcohol group was, overall, more likely to have committed a drug crime of some sort and also to have been processed by the criminal justice system.

SUMMARY AND CONCLUSIONS

This chapter included discussions of a fairly substantial body of data. Because this is the first time that a study like this has been undertaken on alcohol-emergency patients, comparisons are impossible. It is therefore only possible to make a number of general observations and discuss the overall impressions we gathered from these data.

In many ways, the data are suggestive of a skid row-type population. The alcohol-emergency patients are overwhelmingly unemployed, white, male, older, and involved in a pattern of heavy drinking. A very substantial proportion report repeated contact with law enforcement agencies and a significant minority report multiple treatment experiences. Apparently, the treatment itself has not done much for the population, since they either are presenting themselves, once again, at an emergency facility for treatment, or else have been arrested for an offense such as public intoxication.

We can easily conclude, therefore, that this is essentially a damaged population. The question, however, is whether the population is damaged simply because of its alcohol use, or the abuse of beverage alcohol is one component of a broader lifestyle. If the latter is indeed the case, that is, if we are to confirm the lifestyle hypothesis, then a wider range of intervention services is indicated. This would suggest that the hospital emergency room or jail ward, where the bulk of this alcohol-troubled population has come from, should be a place for problem identification. From these facilities, identified members of the problem population could be moved into the service delivery network. However, if this is a skid row or chronic alcoholic population, then the resources required are extensive--units such as residential facilities, halfway houses, and long-term treatment. (For discussion of requirements and problems entailed in treating skid row alcoholics, see NIAAA 1975.)

Future research on alcohol-emergency patients might, therefore, proceed most fruitfully along two major lines. First, subgroup analysis of the kind of survey data reported in this chapter would seem to be helpful. We have emphasized the skid row aspects of our samples, but we have not isolated these people from our total sample for separate analysis. Further, there is also evidence of other kinds of persons being included among these alcohol-emergency patients--most notably women (particularly housewives), a small group of men holding down white-collar or skilled blue-collar jobs, and an even smaller subgroup of people under age 25. Earlier sections of this chapter also indicated that race and ethnicity may be another appropriate subgroup dimension for further analysis.

Finally, we might also recommend that a series of life histories be done on a sample of people seeking treatment for an alcohol-related emergency. This kind of study would provide detailed behavioral and lifestyle data to round out the more general information gathered by survey methodology.

7

CRISIS INTERVENTION AND REFERRAL FOR DRUG-EMERGENCY PATIENTS

Research in drug abuse has typically and repeatedly focused on two generally overlapping sets of people—those who have come to the attention of the criminal justice system and those under treatment in some formal drug rehabilitation program. Indeed, these populations account for a significant portion of those who have become dysfunctional as a result of drug use. Yet, as emphasized throughout this study, there is one unique component of the human-services delivery network geared for the treatment of drug problems that has almost always been ignored—the hospital emergency room.

As explained in Chapter 1, the Acute Drug Reactions Project was designed to address this emergency-room population, with the purpose of not only describing their characteristics and their patterns of drug use but also determining if therapeutic intervention in such a crisis setting would have any impact on their subsequent drug-taking behaviors. Structured around basic crisis intervention theory—that is, the idea of immediate help for a specific problem—it was hypothesized that patients offered therapeutic intervention during a drug-related crisis situation would be more receptive to such intervention in an effort to prevent future drug crises. Clinicians have found that one of the most important variables determining responsiveness to therapy is motivation (see Glasscote et al. 1972). An adverse drug reaction serious enough to require an emergency-room appearance, then, would seem to be a potentially significant motivational factor in making an individual more willing to accept treatment for drug abuse. In short, part of the aim of the ADRP was to experiment with the kind of deliberate change in the treatment delivery system discussed in Chapter 5 as being an apparent necessity. This chapter describes these experimental efforts.

The first two sections describe the setup of the referral system in existence at Jackson Memorial Hospital prior to the beginning of the Acute Drug Reactions Project, and the preliminary survey information gathered by the ADRP in order to set up a new referral system. The next section presents the design of and findings from a followup study done in 1972-73 which explored the consequences of different kinds of intervention attempts with drug-emergency patients. Then, a 1976 followup study of referrals of both drug- and alcohol-emergency patients is described, followed by a discussion of the problems encountered in the referral process and the implications for future research which can be drawn from this part of the Acute Drug Reactions Project.

EXISTING MEDICAL-STAFF
REFERRAL SYSTEM

Prior to the development of an intervention strategy and research design, project researchers examined the existing services and referrals provided by the Jackson Memorial Hospital emergency-room medical staff for drug-emergency patients. The medical emergency-room facilities at Jackson are staffed by permanent nurses and a rotating physician staff of residents, interns, and students. All emergency patients entering the facilities are first seen by the triage nurse for assignment of priority in care and area of treatment (surgery, obstetrics-gynecology, ambulatory care, or medical). Because most drug-involved patients were sent to the medical-emergency area, the investigation of existing treatment referrals for drug users was centered on the medical-emergency wing.

Following the triage procedure a medical-emergency patient will either be seated in the lobby or, in life-threatening cases, be taken into the treatment area for immediate care. When the patient enters this area his vital signs (blood pressure and temperature) are taken by a nurse who then asks preliminary questions about the illness. Subsequent to this initial examination the patient is usually seated in the main hall of the treatment area to await the physician's examination. The waiting period between the initial examination and the first physician's examination is usually 30 minutes to an hour. The physician's examination, in all but the most obvious illnesses, extends over several hours, normally being conducted in segments with lengthy interruptions throughout the examination period.

When the emergency room is busy it takes four to five hours for a patient to be totally processed through the entire system. As the facilities are normally heavily used, the lengthy period of time needed to progress through the medical sequence has several effects on subsequent treatment and referral. First, and most obvious, many patients leave either prior to the initial examination, during the interim period between the initial examination and the physician's examination, or actually during the physician's examination. This leaving "against medical advice" not only terminates medical treatment, but it also effectively denies the patient a referral, whether a medical referral or a social service referral.

Patients managing to complete the medical treatment sequence will frequently refuse a referral, not wanting to delay release or fearing a lengthy wait at any affiliated agency. Again, the lengthy wait decreases the referrals given and accepted.

Finally, the lengthy wait creates an avoidance response to the emergency-room facilities. Patients delay emergency-room visits as long as possible, creating medical situations requiring hospitalization or resulting in death; hospitalization precludes any immediate referral to a drug treatment program or a social service agency.

It was not surprising, then, to find that except for heroin-related cases, very few drug-emergency patients were referred to any service agency. In some selected cases (primarily suicide attempts), short-term crisis intervention sessions were offered to help patients endure the immediate crisis. No long-term help could be provided due to the large number of patients being processed through the hospital psychiatric clinics. Therefore, the approximately 200 patients per month admitted to the emergency room for adverse drug reactions generally received minimal hospital services —services designed to weather the crisis—leaving the patients' underlying psychosocial problems unresolved.

The existing referral efforts of the medical staff were primarily focused upon the heroin users. These patients were routinely referred to the Dade County Comprehensive Drug Program. As described in more detail in Chapter 5, this program is an administrative umbrella organization that channels federal, state, and local funding to a variety of treatment programs providing a wide range of therapeutic and auxiliary services (see Weppner and McBride 1975). The program can be viewed as a model system representing the best of the current varieties of existing traditional treatment structures.

Referrals to drug treatment programs by the medical staff were often given verbally to the patient without a corresponding written referral slip with the name and address of the treatment facilities. The medical staff uses no systematic method for drug referrals, and because these are made routinely they are not always noted on the medical charts. However, the medical files are the most accurate and only available source of medical-staff referrals.

To assess the impact of the existing referral system, the names of 132 heroin-related emergency-room patients who were given a referral to a drug treatment program by the hospital medical staff were compared with the client roster of the Comprehensive Drug Program. All drug users who have applied for admission for treatment in Dade County are included on the Comprehensive Drug Program's data intake logs. Names and corresponding demographic data were compared to determine whether a patient given a medical-staff referral subsequently became a treatment-program client.

As indicated in Table 7.1, the heroin patients who were referred were primarily young adults. Of the 132 cases, over half were aged 18 to 24, and over 90 percent were between 18 and 35 years old. Sex and race were not as concentrated into one category: 57 percent were male; blacks were 43 percent of the referrals, whites 48.5 percent, and Hispanics 8 percent.

TABLE 7.1

Basic Demographic Characteristics of Heroin-Emergency
Patients Referred to Drug Treatment Programs by
Emergency-Room Medical Staff

	Number	Percent
17 and under	3	2.3
18–24	74	56.1
25–34	47	35.4
35–49	8	6.2
50 +	—	—
Male	45	56.8
Female	57	43.2
White	64	48.5
Black	57	43.2
Hispanic	11	8.3
Total	132	100.0

Source: Compiled by the authors.

Of these 132 cases, 51 (38.6 percent) were found to have applied for program admission, while the majority (61.4 percent) had not. Comparison of Table 7.1 to the demographic data on CDP clients (see Chapter 5) suggests that females were particularly unlikely to contact the Comprehensive Drug Program; whites and the 18-24 age group were also slightly underrepresented among CDP patients compared to their percentages among the 132 heroin referrals. In any case, the 38.6 percent contact rate for patients given medical-staff referrals to the CDP is obviously a low one. It indicated the need (and established a baseline figure) for a more active kind of intervention effort in emergency-room referrals to drug treatment programs—even for heroin-involved individuals, who were considerably more likely than other patients to receive any kind of referral at all.

PRELIMINARY STUDIES FOR THE ACUTE
DRUG REACTIONS PROJECT
INTERVENTION STUDY

When the Acute Drug Reactions Project began, in 1972, the referral-intervention phase of the project was concerned with three questions:

▫ What post-emergency-room psychological and social services are most appropriate for various types of drug users?
▫ At what time during the crisis period of a drug reaction is intervention most appropriate and acceptable to patients?
▫ What impact do intervention procedures have on the patient's
▫ post-emergency-room drug-taking activities?

In order to get preliminary information on these questions, former emergency-room drug patients were asked about their service needs, and existing community agencies were surveyed to determine the types and range of programs willing to accept drug-related crisis cases. This information was then used in designing a research study to assess the impact and timing of intervention in regard to subsequent drug use. This section describes the general information gathered in the preliminary surveys.

The survey of former emergency-room patients was begun in order to gather baseline data on individuals who came to the emergency room for treatment of an acute drug reaction during a one-year time period prior to the initiation of the Acute Drug Reaction Project. A sample of 200 prior patients—100 who had experienced acute/adverse reactions to illicit drugs and 100 who had experienced reactions to legally manufactured and distributed drugs—was selected on a random basis. Some 86 legal-drug cases and 72 illicit-drug cases were actually located and interviewed. These interviews provided case histories designed to give information concerning the drugs used, patient drug-use history and reactions, accidental versus deliberate overdosage, the general context in which the drug use occurred, as well as an assessment of the impact of the overdose/drug-reaction experience on the patient's subsequent behavior, lifestyle, and drug-taking activity. Information was also obtained on the nature of the services received during this experience (emergency-room and posthospital experiences), as well as the patients' perceptions of what posthospital services may have been more appropriate to their needs. Both the information and experiences gained from this survey were of considerable value in designing the actual intervention program.

The survey of former acute drug-reactions patients showed that overall they were primarily female, uninvolved in criminal activities, generally housewives who had few educational or occupational skills and who generally could be categorized as involved in a family crisis. It was also found that the drug use that caused the emergency-room appearance was not an isolated episode but rather appeared to be a coping mechanism used by individuals to manage their lives. On the basis of these findings, it was concluded that the emergency-room patients constituted the kind of drug-abusing population which used drugs, particularly sedatives and tranquilizers, to deal with life conflicts, stress, and problems. These findings regarding the extensive abuse of prescription drugs, and the fact that abusers were primarily female and noncriminally involved, both made it quite obvious that referrals to traditional drug treatment programs providing services primarily to male heroin users would be inappropriate. An attempt was therefore made to locate a variety of community organizations which would provide services to the kind of drug abusers seen in a hospital emergency room.

After the study of former drug-reaction patients had been completed, several months were spent in locating the social service agencies in the community that offered appropriate services and were willing to accept referrals of drug-reaction patients from the emergency room. Particular attention was paid to whether or not these programs offered basic educational and vocational training and family support services. On the basis of contacting all such facilities, a list of 25 referral facilities was compiled. Included in this list were the Comprehensive Drug Program and a variety of family counseling programs sponsored by the county, the local mental health board, and various religious groups. A list describing the services offered by each program, its type of staff, location, and contact person was prepared for presentation to patients during the actual intervention and referral phase of the project.

ACTIVE VERSUS PASSIVE INTERVENTION:
A FOLLOWUP STUDY

The basic research question the next aspect of the project attempted to address concerned the impact of intervention upon the patients' willingness to accept treatment referral and cease drug use. To answer this question, a variation of the classical experimental design was used. The study was designed so that comparative analysis could be conducted using three groups selected from among the 1972 drug-emergency patients:

1. Control group: This group had no contact with project interventionists at any time during their hospital care. Whatever intervention services they received were those in existence prior to the initiation of the Acute Drug Reactions Project, and these were, as previously discussed, sporadic and few.
2. Passive intervention group: This group was designed to assess the impact of minimal intervention. Patients in this group were given a pamphlet describing appropriate available services with the telephone numbers of the programs and the names of individuals to contact. On the basis of their service needs a specific program was recommended. No other services were offered.
3. Active intervention group: This group received the services offered the passive group, in addition to which they received a number of other services. These services included:

    □ repeated attempts to encourage the patient to contact a treatment program; the active-intervention patients were contacted a minimum of five times in person at their homes or by telephone;
    □ carefully going over with the patients each of the available programs and discussing their location access by public transportation and hours of operation and services offered;
    □ assisting in arranging for transportation if necessary, so the patient could make contact with a program;
    □ contacting the program the patient chose, making an appointment for the patient, and following up to see if the patient kept the appointment;
    □ offering general support and encouragement to the patient to choose a program and make contact with that program.

The intention was, during a six-month period, to randomly assign all acute drug-reaction patients to each group until there were 100 in each group. However, initial experience in the emergency room indicated that many patients were unconscious or only semiconscious when they came to the emergency room, and left shortly after they regained consciousness, before they could be contacted for an interview. Thus, it was apparent that because of the limited number of staff, many patients would not have the possibility of being included in the study. Rather than lose this group of patients, a decision was made to modify the original design. All of those who could be contacted and interviewed in the hospital were assigned to one of the two intervention groups as planned. Those who could not be contacted in the hospital, however, were also assigned to a passive or active intervention group but were denoted as "field" subjects as opposed to emergency-room subjects since they were contacted in their homes in order to be offered the services designed for that particular group. In addition to keeping more subjects in the study, modification of the design also enabled us to study the effectiveness of referral-intervention during a crisis compared to its effectiveness at a time period following the crisis.

Prior to the actual application of the research design, several weeks were spent in the medical-emergency room observing the patient flow process and gaining the cooperation and support of all levels of the staff. Assuring the cooperation of the staff was essential to the referral project. Indeed, because of the size of the emergency room and the number of individuals (approximately 500) processed through the emergency room on a daily basis, the only way that the project could achieve its aims was through the consistent support and cooperation of the medical care staff. In the initiation of the project, one of the major concerns was the acceptability of the referral-intervention project among the emergency-room staff. One of the pleasant surprises of the project was the acceptance, cooperation, and strong endorsement received from the entire staff. Because drug patients were considered difficult to handle and created problems for the staff, the services of the project interventionists were generally well received. The staff seemed relieved to have someone else deal with individuals whom they considered manipulative, problematic to care for, and "only" suffering from "self-inflicted" difficulties.

At an early stage of the project, time studies were undertaken to determine when the bulk of the drug cases was processed. This information was available from daily records collected by the project on all drug-related admissions on a given day. Analysis was done to discern whether patients with certain types of reactions were more likely to come in during certain times of the day or night, and when the busiest times occurred for drug admissions. Varying patterns were discovered, but because of a limited number of interventionists it was decided to cover the hours when the majority of drug-reaction patients came to the emergency room. It was discovered that the largest percentage of the drug patients could be contacted by covering the emergency room daily from noon to midnight, and on weekends from noon to 3:00 A.M. As the average time for processing a drug patient through the medical- and psychiatric-emergency rooms was over four hours, most morning admissions were still there at noon. Also, many of the late admissions coming in after midnight were held until morning for psychiatric evaluation.

Along with counseling and referral of patients, basic data were collected on each patient for the epidemiological segment of the research. These included basic demographic and pertinent medical data. The patient's perception of the treatment (supportive and traumatic aspects) was included, as well as activities leading to the crisis and how the patient got to the emergency room. The interventionist recorded in some detail the etiology of the problem and a drug history whenever possible. If a referral was made this was recorded, along with the interventionist's perception of the patient's reaction to the referral, and a prognosis.

Providing appropriate postemergency services involved making difficult decisions. Dade County's fairly extensive human-services delivery network meant that appropriate referrals could generally be made, but this was not always the case. Those respondents referred to the hospital's Psychiatric Out-Patient Department (OPD) were, for the most part, unable to be appropriately referred to any other existing agency. Only one illicit-drug case received a referral to the Psychiatric OPD. Referrals for reactions from legal drugs were directed toward community agencies structured around mental health services, since a significant proportion of these were medicine misusers or persons attempting suicide with drugs. Respondents falling into the stereotyped patterns of hard-core drug abusers and suffering from severe psychiatric disorders or suicidal tendencies were referred to drug programs even though such programs did not seek out or desire such clientele. Respondents with the double handicap of severe psychiatric impairment and drug addiction were rejected by psychiatric facilities and drug therapy programs (Weppner and McBride 1974).

As indicated in Table 7.2, 160 cases were included in the study groups. Of these cases, 76 were classified as passive interventions (31 field cases and 45 emergency-room cases) and 84 as active interventions (38 field cases and 46 emergency-room cases).

TABLE 7.2

Subjects for the Active-versus-Passive-Intervention Study: Type of Referral Agency and Legality of Primary Substance Involved, by Intervention Group

	Passive Intervention				Active Intervention			
	Field		Emergency Room		Field		Emergency Room	
	Number	Percent	Number	Percent	Number	Percent	Number	Percent
Community								
Licit	24	77.4	25	55.6	23	60.5	18	39.1
Illicit	—		—		—		1	2.2
Psychiatry Out-Patient Department								
Licit	5	16.1	7	15.6	10	26.3	8	17.4
Illicit	—		1	2.2	—		—	
Comprehensive Drug Program								
Licit	2	6.5	5	11.1	—		13	28.3
Illicit	—		6	13.3	2	5.3	6	13.0
No referral								
Licit	—		1	2.2	3	7.9	—	
Illicit	—		—		—		—	
Total	31		45		38		46	

Source: Compiled by the authors.

Based on the type of drug involved and service needs, 91 cases were referred to community mental health programs, 31 cases were referred to the Psychiatric Out-Patient Department of the University of Miami, and 34 were referred to the Comprehensive Drug Program.

The distribution of referrals reflects primarily the type of drug used and the social characteristics of the patient. Very early in the referral process it was learned that the traditional drug treatment programs are not designed to treat individuals who have abuse problems with legal prescription and over-the-counter drugs and who are not involved in criminal activities (see Weppner et al. 1976). Because of the approach that the treatment programs used (which often emphasized confrontation therapy, the wearing of signs listing misdeeds, and basic personality modification), the licit-drug abusers did not find these types of programs acceptable. Thus, licit-drug patients were referred to the various community mental health programs.*

Some 92 cases were located for followup and interviewed six months after intervention. Respondents were simply asked if they had contacted a referral agency and if they had used the substance that had caused the emergency-room appearance during the subsequent six-month period. Their nonuse of the primary substance was used as the indicator of referral-intervention success. Data are presented in Table 7.3 regarding the proportion of each group who actually made contact with a referral agency. These figures indicate that the individuals in the active emergency-room referral group were the most likely to make contact with an agency. Of the active emergency-room referrals, 64.7 percent made contact, compared to 50 percent of the passive emergency-room referrals, 55 percent of the active field referrals, 37.5 percent of the passive field referrals, and 45.5 percent of the control group. Even though the number of cases was small the difference between the active emergency-room referrals and the control group was statistically significant at the .07 level ($Z = 1.46$).

Data are presented in Table 7.4 showing the percentage of each group who had discontinued use of the substance that had caused the

---

*As researchers have consistently discovered, any attempt to use an experimental design in a natural setting is fraught with hazards. In this study, 21 individuals, most of whom were placed in the control-group category, were lost to the study because they or the medical staff specifically requested intervention services. Rather than deny services when they were requested, it was decided to provide intervention services and remove those 21 individuals from the study population.

TABLE 7.3

Referral-Agency Contacts Made by Followup-Interview Subjects:
The Active-versus-Passive-Intervention Study

| | Passive Intervention | | | | Active Intervention | | | | | |
| | Field | | Emergency Room | | Field | | Emergency Room | | Control Group | |
	Number	Percent	Number	Percent	Number	Percent	Number	Percent	Number	Percent
Agency contact	3	37.5	6	50.0	11	55.0	11	64.7	5	45.5
No agency contact	5	62.5	6	50.0	9	45.0	6	35.3	6	54.5
Total	8	100.0	12	100.0	20	100.0	17	100.0	11	100.0

Source: Compiled by the authors.

TABLE 7.4

Discontinued Use of Primary Substance Involved by Followup-Interview Subjects:
The Active-versus-Passive-Intervention Study

| | Passive Intervention | | | | Active Intervention | | | | | |
| | Field | | Emergency Room | | Field | | Emergency Room | | Control Group | |
	Number	Percent	Number	Percent	Number	Percent	Number	Percent	Number	Percent
Continued use	5	33.3	6	40.0	10	40.0	1	5.9	9	45.0
Discontinued use	10	66.7	9	60.0	15	60.0	16	94.1	11	55.0
Total	15	100.0	15	100.0	25	100.0	17	100.0	20	100.0

Source: Compiled by the authors.

original drug reaction. Once again, the active emergency-room interventions were apparently the most successful referrals. Of the emergency-room active referrals 94.1 percent had discontinued the use of the substance, compared to 60 percent of the passive emergency-room referral group and 55 percent of the control group. While both active and passive field-referral groups were more likely to have discontinued use than the control group, the difference is not statistically significant. Additionally, the passive field-referral group was more likely to have discontinued use (66.7 percent) than the active field-referral group (60 percent) though again the difference was not statistically significant. In fact the active emergency-room referral group was the only group to be significantly more likely to discontinue use than the control group $(Z = 2.60, p < .05)$.

The data presented in Tables 7.3 and 7.4 suggest the importance of intensive referral-intervention services and the timing of those services. The data indicate the positive value of direct and comprehensive referral and counseling services integrated with medical and/or psychiatric services in a hospital setting and, most importantly, services which are available during the crisis period rather than being provided after the crisis has passed. Only those who received active intervention in the emergency room were more likely than the control group to seek and receive counseling services and discontinue drug use.

THE 1976 REFERRAL FOLLOWUP STUDY

The final phase of the ADRP intervention and referral project was designed to investigate the acceptability of existing traditional drug and alcohol treatment programs to a variety of substance-involved persons, including the prescription-drug abuser as well as the illicit-substance abuser. As was noted earlier, it became apparent that traditional treatment programs were only acceptable to a narrow range of drug users—primarily those who used illicit substances. It was the purpose of this phase of the referral project to examine this issue further.

Members of the ADRP staff rotated in the emergency room, extending coverage of the facilities to 16 hours a day, seven days per week. Subjects with drug- or alcohol-related medical or psychiatric problems were interviewed following their discharge from medical care, after which the interviewer made a decision as to the appropriateness of a referral to a drug or alcohol treatment facility. If such a referral was deemed advisable the interviewer briefly outlined the services offered by the Comprehensive Drug

Program and gave the subject a written referral. This written referral was included so as to formalize the referral process and to give the client instructions on how to locate the treatment facility.

The CDP client log was utilized to ascertain whether or not an emergency-room referral client had contacted the CDP for entry into drug treatment. Names of clients as well as associated demographic characteristics were reviewed in order to identify all clients.

All emergency-room referrals were made subsequent to the completion of medical examinations and formal release from the hospital. Patients hospitalized as a result of their acute drug reaction were not interviewed or referred since most would have been unable to follow up on the referral until their release, and further, their physical and mental condition often precluded any contact with them by interviewers. There were also other drug- and alcohol-emergency patients who were not interviewed. Patients were, of course, given the opportunity to refuse the interview and many patients were physically and/or mentally unable to be interviewed even after their release from the emergency room. Finally, since the ADRP staff was limited, patients entering the hospital after 2 A.M. and discharged before 10 A.M. could not be contacted.

The Phase 2 referral system was instituted in March 1976 and continued through May 1976. Referrals were made only to drug and alcohol programs in order to study the relationship between the type of substance abused and acceptability of traditional treatment programs among both illicit- and prescription-drug abusers. The subjects referred by the ADRP were dichotomized into alcohol and drug use in regard to the primary substance responsible for admission. Since the two earlier referral studies—the medical-staff heroin referrals and the active-versus-passive-intervention study—had dealt only with drug patients, alcohol cases were kept separate.

Table 7.5 describes the age, sex, and race and ethnicity for the 51 alcohol patients who were interviewed and thus available for referral during the three-month study period. Not unexpectedly, the drug cases were more often male (59.4 percent) than female (40.6 percent). They were a young adult population with 59.4 percent under age 25 and 87.5 percent under age 35. Some 64.1 percent of these drug cases were white, while 26.6 percent were black and only 9.4 percent were Hispanic. As indicated below, tranquilizers and sedatives were the primary drugs involved in the acute reactions for 57.8 percent (N = 37) of the cases, followed by heroin (12.5 percent) and hallucinogens (6.3 percent):

Drug Involved	N	Percent of Cases
Tranquilizers	19	29.7
Sedatives	18	28.1

Drug Involved	N	Percent of Cases
Stimulants	3	4.7
Narcotics/analgesics	2	3.1
Heroin	8	12.5
Cocaine	1	1.6
Hallucinogens	4	6.3
All other	9	13.1

The alcohol patients, on the other hand, were considerably older, with 59 percent being 35 and above, and even more likely to be male (66.7 percent, versus 59.4 percent of the drug patients). The ethnic distribution was roughly the same, except that Hispanics accounted for only two alcohol patients (4 percent, versus 9.4 percent of the drug patients).

TABLE 7.5

Basic Demographic Characteristics of Alcohol- and Drug-Emergency Patients Interviewed for Possible Referral in the 1976 Followup Study

	Alcohol Cases		Drug Cases	
	Number	Percent	Number	Percent
17 and under	—	—	4	6.3
18–24 years	6	11.8	34	53.1
25–34 years	15	29.4	18	28.1
35–49 years	22	43.1	4	6.3
50+ years	8	15.7	4	6.3
Male	34	66.7	38	59.4
Female	17	33.3	26	40.6
White	34	66.7	41	64.1
Black	15	29.4	17	26.6
Hispanic	2	4.0	6	9.4
Total	51	100.0	64	100.0

Source: Compiled by the authors.

Of the 64 drug patients, referrals were not deemed appropriate in 56.3 percent of the cases. In these instances, the patients had suffered an accidental overdose through the self-medication of a legal drug, and no drug-abuse problem was indicated. Of the remaining 28 drug cases, 24 were referred to the Comprehensive Drug Program—21 to the CDP drug unit and three to the CDP alcohol unit. The remaining four drug cases refused referral. As such, a total of 37.5 percent of the original 64 drug cases were referred. By contrast, 72.5 percent (N = 37) of the alcohol cases were referred to treatment, nine cases were deemed inappropriate for referral, and five alcohol patients refused the referral.

Upon followup 30 days after referral, 61.7 percent (n = 37) of the referred cases were found to have contacted the Dade County Comprehensive Drug Program. More specifically, 56.8 percent (n = 21) of the 37 alcohol cases and 66.7 percent (n = 16) of the 24 drug cases were found to have made use of the referral suggestion. The difference of 10 percent between the drug and alcohol cases may mean that alcohol-emergency patients are less likely to seek treatment than patients experiencing difficulties with other (primarily illicit) substances (but the n's in this study are too small for a difference of this size to be statistically significant).

The drug cases in this study can also be compared to the medical referrals prior to the initiation of the Acute Drug Reactions Project. While 38.6 percent of the heroin patients referred by the medical staff actually contacted the Comprehensive Drug Program, this was true of 66.7 percent of the drug patients referred by project interventionists. These data suggest that even for the traditional illicit-drug users, intervention at the time of a drug crisis may be an important factor in getting that individual to contact a treatment program. Further, written referrals following an interview related to drug-use behavior were apparently considerably more successful in eliciting a subsequent program contact for such individuals than were brief, routine oral referrals.

IMPLICATIONS AND SUGGESTIONS

The intervention and referral strategies utilized in the Acute Drug Reactions Project and the experiences encountered through these phases of the research provide a series of implications and suggestions regarding both followup and referral endeavors.

With respect to followup studies, researchers in the drug-abuse field have been conducting followup studies for more than 30 years, and the literature contains numerous reports concerning the proportion of respondents who are still (or again) using drugs after having left a treatment program. Because the consequent use of drugs following completion of a program is typically viewed as the most significant measure of success, conclusions are then drawn as to the effectiveness of a particular treatment program or technique. Conclusions based on followup studies, however, are potentially biased because researchers often locate only a portion of their subjects, sometimes as few as 50 percent. In addition, researchers often do not report the reasons for their inability to locate all respondents, nor do they discuss the characteristics of those that could not be located. Such a report would be useful to drug professionals for two basic reasons: it would help one to evaluate the validity and utility of the followup data for assessing treatment impact; and it could specify the social and behavioral characteristics of those who can and cannot be located.

In the active-versus-passive intervention study, once the actual intervention part was completed, the staff began a followup study of the referral services. Of the 181 patients ultimately referred, some 45 percent (n = 80) could not be located and interviewed to determine any influences the intervention may have had on their subsequent drug-taking activities and lifestyles. What follows is a brief examination of those who could be located as compared with those who could not, with a view toward the differences between the two which might explain why some could not be located.

Of the patients who could not be located, 77 percent had moved and left no forwarding address, 7 percent had given false addresses, and 17 percent were repeatedly not at home. Those who could not be located were more often white and female, and persons between ages 18 and 35. In addition, the subjects not located were typically users of illicit substances and had not been referred to a treatment agency.

These data suggest some strategies for obtaining a higher proportion of respondents in a followup study. Since the major reason respondents could not be located was that they had moved, researchers should be aware and prepared to spend the time and effort to obtain information from neighbors and friends about where an individual may have relocated and should contact treatment programs or the criminal justice system in that area in an attempt to locate the person. Another strategy may be to enlist the cooperation of a subject at the baseline stage of the interview and urge that individual to keep in contact.

Finally, to facilitate the success of followup studies, there must be adequate preparation at the level of the interventionist's training, for intervention agents are the first and perhaps most crucial contact patients will have with the followup study; and, as they are usually the only nonmedical personnel that patients speak with, intervention agents are in the unique position of being able to offer patients supportive action by taking the time to speak with them about their stressful situation. Because intervention agents are in this unique position, they should be experienced in both counseling and interviewing techniques, and involved in sensitivity, awareness, and communication groups. This will insure a greater reliability of success for followup studies. Community preparation for the followup effort is also desirable, since it can serve to insure grass-roots cooperation in locating the sample patients. In this behalf, field investigators can contact those local agencies and organizations which have a vested interest in the well-being of the community, to explain the nature and importance of the followup, and how the total effort can be enhanced by community support.

In terms of referral implications, the Acute Drug Reactions Project referral system was a more effective method of initiating and assessing treatment contact than were medical-staff referrals to rehabilitation programs. Slightly more than a third (38.6 percent) of the medical-staff referrals made contact with the Comprehensive Drug Program while some two-thirds (66.7 percent) of the Phase 2 ADRP drug referrals made such contact. This greater success may be related to the nature of the intervention as well as the alternative types of drug users encountered. Our experience demonstrated that the interventionists developed better relationships with the emergency-room clients than did the hospital staff. As such, it became apparent that patients were more willing to accept the advice of our project staff. Secondly, the ADRP referrals involved a wide variety of drug-using types—narcotic and nonnarcotic drug users as well as medicine misusers and self-medicators. The hospital staff referred only those patients involved with heroin. It was found that within the wider variety of drug-using types, the emergency-room experience had made many patients suddenly aware that they had a drug problem that they were previously unwilling to recognize, and hence, they were motivated for treatment. This was not necessarily the case for the majority of the heroin users.

The concept of a referral system using a hospital emergency room as a contact site is not a widely utilized outreach mechanism, yet it is a structure within which some significant benefits might be achieved. The emergency room has a somewhat anonymous nature, drawing individuals who have no private physician or who would be averse to contacting their physician about a drug problem. It is a facility used by a broad cross section of society with a variety of drug-related problems, varied in both the nature of the problem and the substance used. The emergency room provides not only new insights as to the nature and extent of drug abuse but the basis for a serious reexamination of the traditional drug treatment network.

In contrasting the emergency-room drug patients with those in the wider human-services delivery network, it was found that the drug-emergency patient was older, more often white and female, and typically a user of the prescription drug. The patient in the formal drug treatment program was more often a male minority group member who was an abuser of illicit substances (see Chapter 5). This suggests that the emergency-room referral system can reach a population that typically fails to come to the attention of other community agencies.

The first phase of the ADRP referral system attempted to deal with this lesser-known drug-using population by providing referrals to community social service agencies as well as to the Comprehensive Drug Program facilities. The problems encountered in this approach were numerous and need to be briefly explained in order to understand the limitations that were placed on the 1976 referral study.

One of the major difficulties encountered in providing referrals to social service agencies was the feedback system. Client confidentiality began to be more strictly enforced, causing a complete breakdown in a system which relied on client contact and progress data from the agencies. Social service agency staff were unwilling and/or unable to verify client contacts with their agency. Information which was initially obtained through informal mechanisms ceased to be available and a formal feedback system could not be achieved. Without agency feedback and progress data, evaluation of the referral process had to be based exclusively on the information provided by subjects during followup, with no mechanism of validation. The only agency willing to provide feedback as to client contact was the Comprehensive Drug Program, which therefore became the only referral agency used during the 1976 study.

An alternative difficulty involved the actual placement of a client. Many social service agencies were unwilling to deal with drug-using clients, and would ultimately rerefer those individuals to a traditional drug treatment program. This occurred even when the client's major problem was understood to be of a "nondrug" nature. Furthermore, for prescription-drug users, there were no appropriate treatment services available.

The need for transportation to social service agencies was a totally unforeseen difficulty encountered by the ADRP staff. Miami, a sprawling metropolitan area, lacks an efficient public transportation system. For many clients an appropriate referral would have required the client to spend several hours commuting if he had no access to an automobile. The ADRP did not have the funds to provide transportation for those needing such a service, and was forced to either make a referral on the basis of geographical propinquity or make no referral.

Many of the community social service agencies in Dade County charge a fee for services rendered. While many potential patients may attach a greater value to a service that requires a cash payment, many were discouraged from using these agencies since the required funds were unavailable to them. As such, clients in this situation failed to make any agency contact.

Based on the experiences of the Acute Drug Reactions Project, an emergency-room-based referral service could represent a significant addition to a community's drug treatment outreach network. The structuring of such a referral service should appropriately include—

1. a full-time emergency-room staff trained in crisis intervention and followup strategies;
2. an initial interview instrument designed to elicit a wide variety of information on client social and personal characteristics and history, combined with extensive information on friends and relatives for locating the client during followup;
3. the structuring of a feedback system for eliciting information on client-agency contact and patient progress in treatment;
4. the structuring of a mechanism for providing funds for transportation to programs, and for subsidizing agency fees; and
5. the establishing of programs for dealing with the prescription-drug users whose problems cannot be addressed by the more traditional drug treatment programs.

8

DRUG-RELATED DEATHS: A 20-YEAR STUDY OF DADE COUNTY, FLORIDA

One of the major public health questions concerning the use of drugs is the extent and nature of the relationship between drugs and death. Often, assessments as to the need for treatment services for particular types of drug use as well as prevalence estimates are based on related death rates. For example, a major part of the evidence used for the nationwide federal effort to establish community drug treatment programs came from data indicating the large number of deaths caused by drugs, particularly heroin (Cherubin et al. 1972; DuPont 1973, 1974; Blair and Sessler 1974). The major focus of this research, however, has generally been confined to number of deaths by substance type--almost completely neglecting attention to the social characteristics of persons dying from use of different substance types. Further, most of these reports deal only or primarily with heroin deaths, while there is a good deal of evidence that many other substances of at least equal dangerousness are being used and abused by far greater numbers of people.

This analysis represents an attempt to examine more fully the relationship between drugs and death, by considering a full range of substance types and major social characteristics of drug-death victims, as well as changes in these factors over a 20-year period. The data collected for this purpose were drawn from Medical Examiner files in Dade County, Florida, for the years 1956-75, and were transferred to a precoded form (Form C in the Appendix). The two types of information included were all substance-related accidental deaths (N = 1,077); and all substance- and nonsubstance-related suicides (N = 4,355).

It should be noted, as many researchers have pointed out, that the accident-versus-suicide classification is often a function of circumstance--whether or not a family physician is present, and despite the opinions of the family, the social characteristics of the person who died, and the specific substance or other factor apparently responsible for the death (see Dublin 1963; Douglas 1967).

131

Under Florida statute, the Medical Examiner is responsible for in-
vestigating all deaths of suspicious, unknown, or violent origins as
well as deaths where no private physician was in attendance. This
means, of course, that there are certain biases in the data used for
this study. Nevertheless, many drug-related deaths are investigated
by the Medical Examiner's office and can provide a useful base for
examining the relationship between drug deaths and social characteristics. Further, most of the data reported in this study can be
usefully considered without regard to the accident-versus-suicide
classification. Since the first two sections of this chapter do use
this classification, however, its possible biases should be kept in
mind while considering the data.

ACCIDENTAL DEATHS

As indicated in Table 8.1, there were some 1,077 substance-
related accidental deaths in Dade County during the period 1956-75.
These included, in addition to deaths involving barbiturates and
other drugs, carbon monoxide poisonings, arsenic poisonings, and
a small number of alcohol-related drownings. The percentage of
these deaths attributable to drugs remained high during the entire
period--varying from 69 percent to 79 percent.

Deaths due to barbiturates alone were generally quite numerous, accounting for 18 percent to 21 percent of these accidental
deaths for most of the period considered, although they dropped to
8.6 percent in 1971-75. At this point, the lethal dangers of barbiturate use have been well documented (see, for example, Setter,
Maher, and Schreiner 1966; Berger 1967). The increased emphasis
by clinicians on these dangers, as well as the greater restriction on
barbiturate production and the development of nonbarbiturate sedatives, doubtless account for some of this decrease.

Another part of the picture, however, is the dramatic increase
in the number of substance-related accidental deaths due to multiple
drugs. From 1956 to 1970, the percentage of deaths due to combinations of drugs was only about 4 percent to 6 percent, but in 1971-75
multiple-drug deaths represented 19.4 percent of the cases. It
might also be noted that there was a consistent decline in the proportion of these cases in which barbiturates were one or more of the
drugs involved: in 1956-60, the figure was 4.0 percent of 4.0 per-
cent--or 100 percent of such cases; in 1961-65, 4.4 percent of 5.8
percent--or 75.9 percent; in 1966-70, 2.6 percent of 4.1 percent--
or 63.4 percent; in 1971-75, 7.2 percent of 19.4 percent--or only
37.1 percent. Both the total and broken-down figures on multiple-
drug deaths provide further support to the work of other researchers

(Kunnes 1973; Lewis 1973; Freedman and Brotman 1969) on the recent major increase in the number and availability of drugs used in
our society. Further, these figures also indicate the need for the
change in conceptions of drug users which has in fact taken place in
recent years, emphasizing multiple-substance use--polydrug use--
rather than attending only to single-substance categories. One consequence of this use pattern, as Table 8.1 may indicate, is that the
interactive effects of drugs upon each other, or in combination with
alcohol, are often not fully known and can thus more readily prove
lethal.

The other major change in substance-related accidental deaths
indicated by the data is the increase in alcohol-related drowning
cases during 1971-75. There were 47 such cases, compared to only
four in the preceding five-year period (11.2 percent versus 1.5 percent) and no cases at all in the earlier years; a change of this magni-
tude is unlikely to be mere happenstance, but the only explanatory
hypothesis which seems immediately reasonable would be that a
change was made in automobile-death classification procedures
(since many of these cases are persons with high alcohol-content
blood tests who were unable to escape when their cars went into
canals or other bodies of water). Finally, it might be noted that the
percentage of deaths reported (in Table 8.1) as due to carbon monoxide poisoning decreased during 1971-75 to about 13 percent from the
earlier figures of 21 percent or more. The number of such deaths,
however, is not that different during the four subperiods (52, 44, 59,
and 53 for the respective five-year categories), indicating that the
apparent recent decrease is more likely to be simply an artifact of
the actual increases in other types of substance-related accidental
deaths--most notably deaths due to multiple drugs, as well as the
alcohol-related drownings.

SUICIDE TRENDS

Table 8.2 shows that drugs accounted for a sizable number of
the 4,355 total suicide cases in Dade County for the 20-year period,
even considering nonsubstance- as well as substance-related suicides. The most frequent single cause of death in all four subperiods was a gunshot, which accounted for about a third of all suicides. Combining the three drug categories, however, the number
of drug-related suicides is roughly the same as the number of gunshot
cases for 1961 through 1975.

Trends shown in these data echo those from the accidental-
death data. Specifically, the most consistent and dramatic change
over the 20 years was the increase in suicides by multiple drugs--

TABLE 8.1

Substance-Related Accidental Deaths, Dade County, Florida, 1956-75
(percent)

Cause of Death	1956-60 (N = 177)	1961-65 (N = 208)	1966-70 (N = 274)	1971-75 (N = 418)
Barbiturates	18.1	20.7	20.1	8.6
Other single drugs, chemicals	46.9	52.4	51.3	47.8
Multiple drugs	4.0	5.8	4.1	19.4
Carbon monoxide	29.4	21.2	21.5	12.7
Poisons	1.7	.0	1.5	.2
Alcohol drowning	.0	.0	1.5	11.2

Source: Compiled by the authors.

TABLE 8.2

Suicides, Dade County, Florida, 1956-75
(percent)

Cause of Death	1956-60 (N = 772)	1961-65 (N = 1,039)	1966-70 (N = 1,134)	1971-75 (N = 1,410)
Barbiturates	16.8	23.6	21.9	16.4
Other single drugs, chemicals	5.4	9.1	9.9	9.7
Multiple drugs	.1	2.9	3.3	7.9
Carbon monoxide	18.1	11.3	7.8	5.9
Poisons	2.7	1.6	1.9	.9
Alcohol drowning	.4	.2	.7	.4
Plastic bags	.6	.3	.8	.9
Fire	.8	.6	.9	.9
Hanging	11.1	8.4	7.3	10.5
Gunshot	34.5	31.8	34.2	34.8
Drowning	5.6	4.6	4.7	4.3
Stabbing	1.2	2.0	2.3	1.8
Jumping	2.6	3.4	4.4	5.9

Source: Compiled by the authors.

from only one such case in 1956-60, to about 3 percent in 1961-70, and then to almost 8 percent of all suicides in 1971-75. The data also show a decrease in suicides by barbiturate drugs from the 1961-70 period (22 percent-24 percent) to the 1971-75 years (16.4 percent). Partly because of the suicide-accident classification difficulty, but also because of the overall increased trend toward polydrug use and the changes in barbiturates versus other drugs that have been documented by other researchers, one would expect to find--as these data in fact show--evidence of both trends in the suicide as well as the accident deaths.

The other substance-related trend shown in Table 8.2 is a consistent decrease in the proportion of suicides attributable to nondrug substances. This is particularly obvious for carbon monoxide-related suicides, which decreased in percentage of all suicides by about a third in each of the four periods, going from 18 percent of the 1956-60 cases to about 6 percent of the 1971-75 cases. (And, unlike the accident cases, these decreases also represent decreases in numbers.) The same pattern can be seen on a much smaller scale for suicide by poisons--going from 2.7 percent in 1956-60 to 1.6 percent and 1.9 percent in the two following periods, and then to only 0.9 percent (N = 13) in 1971-75. There is no ready explanation for either decrease. One might suspect, however, that the comparative difficulty of carrying out a suicide of another type might mean a preference for easier or faster methods. This guess does at least agree with many recent analyses of changes in American culture (the wish for instant results, greater general reluctance to plan ahead, and so forth), but it remains only a guess and the data indicate no obvious increase in some other type of suicide which might have come to serve as an easier alternative.

Before proceeding to a look at the social characteristics of substance-related death victims, a final note on the general suicide and accident trends might be in order. Specifically, Tables 8.1 and 8.2 could be compared in terms of how many deaths for each substance type were suicides versus accidents. Sufficient information is given in the tables to permit the reader to do this, but it is not done in this study because of the methodological vagaries in classification previously mentioned. For the same reason, the remainder of this chapter deals with suicides and accidental deaths considered together. (For theoretical reasons for considering them together, see Inciardi, McBride, and Pottieger 1978.)

DRUG CLASSIFICATIONS USED IN THIS CHAPTER

The remainder of this chapter deals only with drug-related deaths and uses the following categories for classifying drugs:

□ Narcotics and analgesics: the pain-relieving drugs other than heroin
□ Heroin
□ Sedatives and tranquilizers: barbiturate and nonbarbiturate sedatives, and major and minor tranquilizers
□ Amphetamines and stimulants: all types of amphetamines and such nonamphetamine stimulants as Nitalin or Dexedrine
□ Cocaine
□ Inhalants: all types of solvents and vapors
□ Hallucinogens: including LSD and hashish
□ Other: all other drugs, which include many different types of medicines--primarily over-the-counter drugs, antibiotics, and metabolic medicines

DRUG-RELATED DEATHS AND AGE

The data presented in Table 8.3 show several consistencies throughout the 1956-75 period in the relationship between age and type of drug causing death. One of these is that sedatives and tranquilizers were the single most important drug type in drug-related deaths among persons 25 years old or older. Further, in three of the four subperiods, the percentage of each age group for whom drug-related deaths were due to sedatives or tranquilizers consistently increased by age category. Another consistent pattern is that for persons 17 years old and younger, the largest category for drug-related deaths was, for all four subperiods, other drugs. These deaths were primarily those of children who had found and used various medicines and over-the-counter drugs in their homes.

A number of changes between 1956 and 1975 in the relation between age and drug deaths are also reflected in these data. The most dramatic is the increase in drug deaths among persons in the 18-24 age category. In 1956-60, only one drug-related death was reported for this age category, followed by 35 in 1961-65, 73 in 1966-70, and finally, 104 in 1971-75. As percentages of total deaths, then, the 18-24 age group accounted for 0.4 percent, 7.2 percent, 12.8 percent, and 17.2 percent in the respective five-year periods (see the bottom line on Table 8.3). Looking at which particular drugs were involved in this increase, it can be noted that the other-drugs category consistently declined throughout the period, while major increases occurred--in sporadic fashion relative to each other--first for the sedatives and tranquilizers (which accounted for 65.7 percent of the drug-related deaths for this age group in 1961-65) and then for heroin (46.6 percent in 1966-70 and, adding analgesics and other narcotics besides heroin, 54.8 percent in this period).

TABLE 8.3

Substance Causing Drug-Related Deaths by Age Group and Year of Death*

(percent)

	1956–60					1961–65				
	17 and under N = 22	18–24 N = 1	25–34 N = 35	35–49 N = 115	50 and over N = 110	17 and under N = 30	18–24 N = 35	25–34 N = 45	35–49 N = 139	50 and over N = 238
Narcotics and analgesics	--	--	--	--	.9	--	2.9	2.2	--	1.3
Heroin	--	--	2.9	.9	--	--	--	2.2	--	.4
Sedatives and tranquilizers	--	--	51.4	66.1	60.0	13.3	65.7	75.6	65.5	73.5
Amphetamines and stimulants	27.3	--	11.4	.9	2.7	56.7	8.6	4.4	4.3	3.4
Cocaine	--	--	--	--	--	--	--	--	--	--
Inhalants	--	--	2.9	--	1.8	--	--	2.2	--	1.3
Hallucinogens	--	--	--	--	--	--	--	--	--	.4
Other	72.7	100.0	31.4	32.2	34.5	30.0	22.9	15.6	30.2	19.7
Total	7.8	.4	12.4	40.6	38.9	6.2	7.2	9.2	28.5	48.9

	1966–70					1971–75				
	17 and under N = 27	18–24 N = 73	25–34 N = 74	35–49 N = 145	50 and over N = 250	17 and under N = 28	18–24 N = 104	25–34 N = 81	35–49 N = 120	50 and over N = 270
Narcotics and analgesics	--	8.2	10.8	2.8	1.6	21.4	14.4	14.8	4.2	2.6
Heroin	14.8	46.6	23.0	2.8	--	7.1	38.5	23.5	2.5	--
Sedatives and tranquilizers	11.1	30.1	51.4	72.4	78.0	21.4	34.6	44.4	65.0	75.9
Amphetamines and stimulants	25.9	2.7	4.1	2.8	4.4	--	2.9	1.2	1.7	1.5
Cocaine	--	--	1.4	.7	--	--	1.0	3.7	--	--
Inhalants	11.1	--	2.7	--	--	10.7	1.9	--	--	--
Hallucinogens	--	--	--	--	--	--	--	--	.8	--
Other	37.0	12.3	6.7	18.6	16.0	39.3	6.7	12.3	25.8	20.0
Total	4.7	12.8	13.0	25.5	43.9	4.6	17.2	13.4	19.9	44.8

*Information as to age of 45 individuals was missing.
Source: Compiled by the authors.

The overall pattern of changes in the association between age and deaths from sedatives and tranquilizers, however, looks somewhat different from that for deaths from heroin. With sedatives and tranquilizers, number of deaths in the 18-24 age group rose after the 1961-65 appearance of this category, but not dramatically; as a percentage of these drug-related deaths, it was considerably lower after 1961-65--only about half the 65.7 percent figure. In fact, it looks as if the 1966-75 figures for all age groups indicate a filtering down in the availability of these drugs. During the whole decade, deaths from sedatives and tranquilizers occurred for the entire range of age groups--17 and under through 50 and over--and showed steady increases with age.

The pattern for age and deaths from heroin, on the other hand, shows almost all deaths being for people under 35 and shows a peak in the 1966-70 period. Even for persons 17 and under, deaths from heroin accounted for almost 15 percent of the cases in this period-- compared to none in the preceding ten years and about 7 percent in 1971-75. For persons over 24, there were only four deaths from heroin in the entire decade preceding 1966-70; in 1966-70, however, there were 21 such deaths and in 1971-75 there were 22--in both periods representing about 23 percent of the drug-related deaths among persons 25-34 (compared to 47 percent and 39 percent in the respective periods for the 18-24 age group). Only seven of these 43 deaths were for persons over 34, so that for the decade as a whole, heroin deaths represent only 2.6 percent of the cases for the 35-49 age group. Finally, it might also be noted that only one heroin death for someone in the 50-and-over group was recorded for the entire 20-year span. In short, what these age differences and changes over time appear to show is the occurrence of the "heroin epidemic" among young people which researchers reported as happening during the late 1960s (see McGrath and Scarpitti 1967). The data also indicate, however, that even though heroin use has apparently not increased during the 1970s, it remains a major problem among young people-- especially those 18 to 24, but also among 25-34-year-olds.

A final pattern which may be indicated by these data relates to cocaine. No deaths from cocaine were reported until the 1966-70 period, when two were reported, followed by four in 1971-75. These are, of course, very small numbers; but they are indicative of the recent increased fashionableness of cocaine use, and it might be noted that three of these six deaths occurred in the 25-34 age group.

DRUG-RELATED DEATHS AND RACE/ETHNICITY

The most prominent characteristic of the relationship between drug-related deaths and race/ethnicity is, as indicated in Table 8.4,

TABLE 8.4

Substance Causing Drug-Related Deaths by Race/Ethnicity and Year of Death*
(percent)

	1956-60				1961-65			
	White N = 246	Black N = 35	Hispanic N = 2	Other N = 2	White N = 411	Black N = 62	Hispanic N = 14	Other N = 0
Narcotics and analgesics	.4	--	--	--	.7	--	--	--
Heroin	--	5.7	--	--	.2	1.6	7.1	--
Sedatives and tranquilizers	65.0	20.0	--	--	76.4	6.5	64.3	--
Amphetamines and stimulants	2.8	--	--	--	3.6	33.9	--	--
Cocaine	--	--	--	--	--	--	--	--
Inhalants	.8	5.7	--	--	.5	3.2	--	--
Hallucinogens	--	--	--	--	.2	--	--	--
Other	30.9	68.6	100.0	100.0	18.3	54.8	28.6	--
Total	86.3	12.3	.7	.7	84.4	12.7	2.9	--

	1966-70				1971-75			
	White N = 469	Black N = 57	Hispanic N = 42	Other N = 2	White N = 489	Black N = 74	Hispanic N = 38	Other N = 2
Narcotics and analgesics	4.3	1.8	2.4	--	7.8	8.1	2.6	--
Heroin	6.6	21.1	38.1	--	5.3	44.6	13.2	--
Sedatives and tranquilizers	72.3	15.8	35.7	50.0	68.9	8.1	44.7	50.0
Amphetamines and stimulants	2.6	24.6	2.4	--	1.2	2.7	5.3	--
Cocaine	--	3.5	--	--	.6	--	2.6	--
Inhalants	.9	1.8	--	--	.8	1.4	2.6	--
Hallucinogens	--	--	--	--	--	--	--	--
Other	13.4	31.5	21.4	50.0	15.3	35.1	28.9	50.0
Total	82.3	10.0	7.4	.4	81.1	12.3	6.3	.4

*Information as to the race/ethnicity of 42 individuals was missing.

Source: Compiled by the authors.

that over 80 percent of these deaths were for whites. Blacks accounted for 10-13 percent of the cases in each period, while the percentage of Hispanics increased from 1-3 percent in the first ten years considered in the study to 6-7 percent in the more recent decade (which probably reflects the migration of Cubans to Miami that began in 1960). Because the Medical Examiner's office is often viewed as dealing with only indigent and minority groups, the 80 percent-plus figures for whites may appear surprising. The data indicate, however, that most of the drug-related deaths for whites are not from drugs associated with street use, but rather, from prescription drugs. From 65 percent to 77 percent of the white deaths in each five-year period were from sedatives and tranquilizers, with the majority of the remaining deaths being from the medicines and over-the-counter substances classified as other drugs.

These data also show, however, that white deaths represented a slowly but consistently decreasing percentage of drug-related deaths over the 20-year span—primarily, but not solely, due to the increased number of Hispanic drug deaths. That is, percentage of white deaths continued to fall from 1966-70 to 1971-75, but the percentage (and total number) of Hispanic deaths also fell slightly between these two periods.

The major drug apparently responsible for increased minority group drug deaths was heroin. In 1966-70, the period which saw the dramatic increase in the number of heroin-related deaths, heroin accounted for 21 percent of the black and 38 percent of the Hispanic cases; in 1971-75, it was involved in almost 45 percent of the black drug-related deaths as well as 13 percent of the Hispanic cases (a large drop from the preceding period—from 16 to five cases). Thus, while deaths from heroin apparently peaked during the late 1960s, heroin-epidemic years for both whites and Hispanics, the data show that the percentage (and the number) of black heroin-related deaths continued to increase into the 1970s. The number and age of persons dying from heroin did not continue to increase, then, but the racial identity of heroin victims did change between 1966-70 and 1971-75, to become, more than ever, a black problem.

Finally, the race/ethnicity information in Table 8.4 also shows that sedatives and tranquilizers became increasingly prominent in drug-related deaths for Hispanics over the 20 years considered in the study. From no such deaths before 1961, sedative- and tranquilizer-related deaths for Hispanics increased to nine in 1961-65, 15 in 1966-70, and 17 in 1971-75. Thus, heroin was not the only drug responsible for increased minority group deaths over the 20-year span.

DRUG-RELATED DEATHS AND SEX

Overall, sex differences were not as important as differences in age or race/ethnicity in drug-related deaths. As indicated in Table 8.5, males and females were fairly equally represented in the drug-related death population. And, for three of the four periods, sedatives and tranquilizers accounted for over half the drug-related deaths for both sexes, with the other-drugs category making up another 15-to-25 percent of the total.

There were, however, several noticeable differences in relation to specific drug types. The biggest relative difference is for heroin, with the male-to-female ratio running from over two-to-one up to almost four-to-one in the heroin-peak years of the late 1960s. Males also had more deaths due to cocaine, amphetamines, and other stimulants than did females, although the total number of such deaths is relatively small. With sedatives and tranquilizers, however, where the numbers are quite large, there is also a consistent difference by sex. In every period, female deaths from these drugs outnumbered male deaths from them, and the ranges for all periods considered do not even overlap--that for females being 68.5-75.2 percent and the range for males being 38.5-61.1 percent.

The information in Table 8.5 can also be used to further elaborate the previous data regarding the 1966-70 increase in heroin deaths. The percentage of drug-related deaths due to heroin increased dramatically from the 1961-65 figures for both sexes--from 0.9 percent to 16.7 percent for males and from 0.4 percent to 4.2 percent for females--but the jump was almost twice as large for males. Added to the previous information on this change, then, the population most at risk of death from heroin during the 1966-70 peak were minority group males under age 35 and especially black males under 25.

Finally, the sex data from this study can also be used to look at the more general phenomenon of an overall increase in drug use during the 1960s and continuing into the 1970s. Specifically, the biggest increase responsible for the jump between 1956-60 and 1961-65 was that of deaths from sedatives and tranquilizers, among males particularly but also among females. In 1956-60, there were 103 female and 57 male deaths from sedatives and tranquilizers; for 1961-65 the numbers were 192 females and 135 males; and there has been no sign of a decrease since then. Secondly, the periods which saw a large increase in the number of drug-related deaths among people aged 18 to 24 were also those in which a slight but consistent increase in drug-related deaths among males appeared-- from 45 percent of all drug-related deaths in 1961-65 to 49 percent for 1966-70, and continuing to 52 percent for 1971-75.

TABLE 8.5

Substance Causing Drug-Related Deaths by Sex and Year of Death*
(percent)

	1956-60 Male N = 148	1956-60 Female N = 137	1961-65 Male N = 221	1961-65 Female N = 266	1966-70 Male N = 281	1966-70 Female N = 289	1971-75 Male N = 314	1971-75 Female N = 289
Narcotics and analgesics	.7	--	.9	.4	5.7	2.1	7.3	7.6
Heroin	1.4	--	.9	.4	16.7	4.2	14.3	6.6
Sedatives and tranquilizers	38.5	75.2	61.1	72.2	52.3	75.1	51.9	68.5
Amphetamines and stimulants	6.8	2.9	10.0	5.3	7.1	2.4	1.9	1.4
Cocaine	--	--	--	--	.4	.3	1.3	--
Inhalants	2.0	.7	.9	.8	1.1	.7	1.6	.3
Hallucinogens	--	--	.5	--	--	--	--	--
Other	50.7	21.2	25.8	21.0	16.7	15.2	21.7	15.6
Total	51.9	48.1	45.4	54.6	49.3	50.7	52.1	47.9

*Information as to the sex of 42 individuals was missing.

Source: Compiled by the authors.

DRUG-RELATED DEATHS AND MARITAL STATUS

The differences found in drug-related deaths broken down by marital status, reported in Table 8.6, appear to be primarily reflections of age differences between married (or formerly married) and never-married persons. Thus, the never-married category-- as was generally the case for the under-25 age groups--is usually the one category that does not show about two-thirds to three-fourths of the drug-related deaths in a given period as being due to sedatives and tranquilizers. Similarly, the heroin increase of the late 1960s appears most strongly in the never-married category, accounting for 24-25 percent of all drug-related deaths in the 1966-75 decade, compared to about 7 percent for married persons, 3-4 percent for divorced persons, and none at all for the 169 widowed persons who died from drugs during this period. Further, the one marital-status category showing a consistent change pattern over the 20 years was, again, the never-married category, for which (as with young people in general) there was a steady increase in size relative to the other categories--from 20.4 percent of all drug-related deaths in 1956-60 to 30.7 percent in 1971-75. And, finally, the consistently large percentage of the drug deaths attributable to widowed persons (considering their relatively small proportion of the general population) can be seen as a function of the large number of persons over 50 in the drug-death population (39-49 percent of all drug deaths, as reported in Table 8.3).

DRUG-RELATED DEATHS AND OCCUPATION

Table 8.7 shows the relationship between drug-related deaths and type of occupation. It indicates, as hinted in the race/ethnicity data, that drug-related deaths occur in a broad spectrum of the general population. Only about 16-18 percent of the deaths occurred among unskilled or service workers, and the percentage of deaths attributable to the unemployed never rose over 2.4 percent. In fact, of the broad categories listed in Table 8.7, the one which consistently shows the highest percentage of drug deaths in any given period is that of housewives--for them, sedatives and tranquilizers were the drug in question for some 76-85 percent of the cases, with almost all the rest being from the "other" (over-the-counter and general medicinal) drugs. The other general pattern displayed by these data is a great deal of consistency throughout the various periods in the percentage of drug deaths occurring in each occupational group.

TABLE 8.6

Substance Causing Drug-Related Deaths by Marital Status and Year of Death*
(percent)

1956-60

	Common Law N = 0	Married N = 123	Divorced N = 53	Separated N = 0	Widowed N = 43	Never Married N = 56
Narcotics and analgesics	--	.8	--	--	--	--
Heroin	--	1.6	--	--	--	--
Sedatives and tranquilizers	--	67.5	64.2	--	69.8	21.4
Amphetamines and stimulants	--	4.9	--	--	--	14.3
Cocaine	--	--	--	--	--	--
Inhalants	--	.8	1.9	--	2.3	--
Hallucinogens	--	--	--	--	--	--
Other	--	24.4	34.0	--	27.9	64.3
Total	--	44.7	19.3	--	15.6	20.4

1961-65

	Common Law N = 4	Married N = 271	Divorced N = 63	Separated N = 1	Widowed N = 71	Never Married N = 104
Narcotics and analgesics	--	1.2	--	--	--	--
Heroin	--	.4	1.6	--	--	1.0
Sedatives and tranquilizers	--	68.0	77.8	100.0	76.1	54.8
Amphetamines and stimulants	--	4.1	1.6	--	4.2	21.2
Cocaine	--	--	--	--	--	--
Inhalants	--	.8	--	--	1.4	1.0
Hallucinogens	--	.4	--	--	--	--
Other	100.0	25.0	19.0	--	18.3	22.1
Total	.8	49.8	13.0	.2	14.7	21.5

1966-70

	Common Law N = 1	Married N = 246	Divorced N = 91	Separated N = 4	Widowed N = 71	Never Married N = 148
Narcotics and analgesics	--	4.5	3.3	--	--	5.4
Heroin	--	7.3	4.4	--	--	25.0
Sedatives and tranquilizers	100.0	68.3	75.8	75.0	76.1	43.9
Amphetamines and stimulants	--	4.5	2.2	--	5.6	6.8
Cocaine	--	.4	--	--	--	.7
Inhalants	--	.8	--	--	--	2.0
Hallucinogens	--	--	--	--	--	--
Other	--	14.2	14.3	25.0	18.3	16.2
Total	.2	43.9	16.2	.7	12.7	26.4

1971-75

	Common Law N = 0	Married N = 207	Divorced N = 96	Separated N = 7	Widowed N = 98	Never Married N = 181
Narcotics and analgesics	--	4.8	8.3	14.3	3.1	12.2
Heroin	--	6.8	3.1	14.3	--	24.9
Sedatives and tranquilizers	--	68.1	65.6	42.9	78.6	39.2
Amphetamines and stimulants	--	1.4	--	14.3	1.0	2.8
Cocaine	--	.5	--	--	--	1.7
Inhalants	--	--	1.0	--	--	2.8
Hallucinogens	--	--	--	--	--	--
Other	--	18.4	21.9	14.3	17.3	16.5
Total	--	35.1	16.3	1.2	16.6	30.7

*Information on the marital status of 48 individuals was missing.

Source: Compiled by the authors.

TABLE 8.7

Substance Causing Drug–Related Deaths by Occupation and Year of Death*
(percent)

1956–60

	Professional-Technical/Managerial-Administrative N = 53	Sales/Clerical N = 34	Skilled/Semiskilled N = 37	Unskilled/Service N = 51	Housewife N = 80	Unemployed N = 2	Student N = 23
Narcotics and analgesics	--	--	2.7	3.9	--	--	--
Heroin	--	--	--	--	--	--	--
Sedatives and tranquilizers	71.7	79.4	43.2	21.6	82.5	50.0	4.3
Amphetamines and stimulants	3.8	--	--	9.8	1.3	--	26.1
Cocaine	--	--	--	--	--	--	--
Inhalants	1.9	--	2.7	2.0	--	--	--
Hallucinogens	--	--	--	--	--	--	--
Other	22.6	20.6	51.4	62.7	16.2	50.0	69.6
Total	18.9	12.1	13.2	18.2	28.6	.7	8.2

1961–65

	Professional-Technical/Managerial-Administrative N = 79	Sales/Clerical N = 66	Skilled/Semiskilled N = 51	Unskilled/Service N = 81	Housewife N = 155	Unemployed N = 7	Student N = 44
Narcotics and analgesics	2.5	--	2.0	--	.6	--	--
Heroin	--	1.5	--	1.2	--	--	--
Sedatives and tranquilizers	86.1	87.9	49.0	44.4	76.1	57.1	31.8
Amphetamines and stimulants	1.3	3.0	7.8	8.6	3.2	--	38.6
Cocaine	--	--	--	--	--	--	--
Inhalants	1.3	--	--	2.5	.6	--	--
Hallucinogens	1.3	--	--	--	--	--	--
Other	7.6	7.6	41.2	43.2	19.4	42.9	29.5
Total	16.4	13.7	10.6	16.8	32.1	1.4	9.1

1966-70

	Professional-Technical/Managerial-Administrative N = 103	Sales/Clerical N = 72	Skilled/Semiskilled N = 74	Unskilled/Service N = 93	Housewife N = 162	Unemployed N = 9	Student N = 49
Narcotics and analgesics	3.9	1.4	2.7	9.7	1.9	--	6.1
Heroin	4.9	4.2	14.9	25.8	1.2	--	28.6
Sedatives and tranquilizers	73.8	81.9	51.4	33.3	84.6	66.7	22.4
Amphetamines and stimulants	2.9	1.4	6.8	7.5	.6	22.2	16.3
Cocaine	--	--	--	2.2	--	--	--
Inhalants	1.0	--	--	--	.6	--	6.1
Hallucinogens	--	--	--	--	--	--	--
Other	13.6	11.1	24.3	21.5	11.1	11.1	20.4
Total	18.3	12.8	13.2	16.5	28.8	1.6	8.7

1971-75

	Professional-Technical/Managerial-Administrative N = 117	Sales/Clerical N = 79	Skilled/Semiskilled N = 80	Unskilled/Service N = 94	Housewife N = 140	Unemployed N = 14	Student N = 60
Narcotics and analgesics	4.3	3.8	6.3	9.6	5.0	--	21.7
Heroin	7.7	5.1	11.2	26.6	.7	28.6	18.3
Sedatives and tranquilizers	73.5	74.7	55.0	30.9	80.0	50.0	26.7
Amphetamines and stimulants	2.6	2.5	1.3	2.1	.7	--	1.7
Cocaine	1.7	--	--	1.1	--	--	1.7
Inhalants	--	1.3	--	2.1	--	--	5.0
Hallucinogens	--	--	--	--	--	--	--
Other	10.3	12.7	26.2	27.7	13.6	21.4	25.0
Total	20.0	13.5	13.7	16.1	24.0	2.4	10.3

*Information as to the occupational status of 78 individuals was missing.
Source: Compiled by the authors.

147

Where differences and changes appear, however, is in type of drug implicated in the deaths. The major difference in this factor is between white-collar and blue-collar occupations. For professional-technical and managerial-administrative workers, as well as sales and clerical workers, sedatives and tranquilizers account for over 70 percent of the drug-related deaths, with the other-drug category comprising most of the rest of the cases. But for skilled, semi-skilled, and unskilled or service workers, the pattern was both different from that for white-collar workers and different over time. In the first decade studied, 1956-65, 88-95 percent of all drug deaths for blue-collar workers were due to the same prescription and other-drug categories prominent for white-collar workers, but with roughly 40-to-60 percent of the cases being in the other-drug category, compared to roughly 10-to-20 percent for white-collar deaths. Then for the second decade, 1966-75, heroin began to account for 11-15 percent of the skilled-semiskilled worker drug deaths and 26-27 percent of the unskilled-service worker drug deaths. This was a much more significant change than that reflected for the white-collar workers, since even in the peak years of 1966-70 heroin-related deaths never came to as many as 7 percent of white-collar drug-related deaths.

A final type of analysis permitted by these occupational data is observation of changes in drug-related deaths for students. While representing the consistently smallest category (except for the un-employed) for every period, the numbers for students are large enough to permit one to see a real increase in the number of student drug-related deaths--from 23 in 1956-60 to 44 in 1961-65, then to 49, and finally to 60 cases in 1971-75. This increase not only kept pace with the increase for drug-related deaths as a whole, but ac-tually exceeded it since student deaths accounted for a slightly in-creased proportion of all drug-related deaths over the 20 years. More striking is the change in type of drug responsible for student drug deaths. In the late 1950s, the breakdown of drugs responsible was 70 percent "other" drugs, 26 percent amphetamines and other stimulants, and 4 percent (one case) sedatives/tranquilizers. In 1961-65, however, sedatives and tranquilizers accounted for almost a third of all student deaths; deaths from amphetamines and stimu-lants had also increased (to 39 percent), but the number of other-drug cases stayed about the same and thus represented only about 30 percent of all student drug-related deaths. Still, only these three drug types were represented. In 1966-70, however, deaths were also recorded for narcotics and analgesics (6 percent), inhalants (6 percent), and--accounting for the biggest change--heroin (28.6 percent). All six categories continued to appear into 1971-75, and still another was added, due to one student death related to cocaine. The changes in student drug-related deaths between 1966-70 and

1971-75 were, furthermore, not very large. The percentage of deaths due to sedatives and tranquilizers increased slightly (from 22 percent to 27 percent), as did deaths related to the "other" category (20 percent to 25 percent). While heroin-related deaths seemed to decrease between these periods (from almost 29 percent in the late 1960s to about 18 percent in the early 1970s), it should be noted that deaths related to the other-narcotics-plus-analgesics categories increased greatly at the same time (from 6 percent to 22 percent), so that the number of deaths due to narcotics of any sort probably stayed roughly the same or even increased. The one drug type which did show a dramatic and definite change between these periods was amphetamines and other stimulants--from 16 percent in 1966-70 (itself a big drop from the 1961-65 figure of 39 percent) to only one case (1.7 percent) in 1971-75. This change probably reflects both the increased student acceptance of the "Speed kills" motto--referring to the danger of methamphetamine use--and a change in student drug preferences in general since, it will be recalled, amphetamines and other stimulants had represented more than a fourth of student drug-related deaths even in 1961-65.

SUMMARY

The data discussed in this chapter, drawn from 20 years of Medical Examiner office records, display several consistencies throughout the period examined. Most importantly, they show that drug-related deaths tend to be deaths of whites, deaths related to prescription drugs, and deaths of both males and females. They also tend to be more frequent among older people and quite well distributed throughout the socioeconomic spectrum.

The data can also be summarized as showing four major trends in drug-related deaths between 1956 and 1975. First, records on both accidental deaths and suicides indicate that deaths due to barbiturates decreased, compared to both 1961-65 and 1966-70, in the 1971-75 period. Second, the same two sets of records also indicate that 1971-75 saw an increase in deaths from multiple drugs. Third, evidence is displayed of the existence of a heroin epidemic in the 1966-70 period--a dramatic increase in heroin-related deaths from prior years, followed by a smaller but noticeable decline in the 1971-75 period. This epidemic apparently had the greatest effect on persons aged 18 to 24, males, minority groups, the never-married, and both unskilled or service workers and students. Fourth, these data indicate that sedatives and tranquilizers have become a significant danger to increasing numbers of population subgroups--men in general, as well as the 18-24 age group, beginning in the early 1960s; Hispanics, in the same time period, followed by another large increase for them in 1971-75; and persons 17 and under, again beginning in the 1960s and then increasing markedly in 1971-75. Some of these increases, it should be noted, occurred during the period--the early 1970s--when other evidence indicates a decline in deaths due to barbiturates. Further, it is important to note that both barbiturate and nonbarbiturate sedatives are much more toxic, in terms of dose required to cause death, than even the major tranquilizers. Hence, these increases--and the consistently high number of deaths for women, whites, and persons over 25 attributable to sedatives and tranquilizers--would seem to come from two factors: recent increased use of nonbarbiturate sedatives and combinations of various sedatives with other drugs.

The single most important conclusion which can be drawn from the data presented in this chapter, then, is that the biggest drug-related death problem comes from prescription drugs. Sedatives and tranquilizers are the single most important cause of death in such cases for most subgroups over age 25; the second most frequent category for the same subgroups--and the number-one category for persons 17 and under--is that of miscellaneous over-the-counter and prescribed medicinal drugs. In short, while heroin takes an appalling number of lives, sedatives and other perfectly legal drugs take even more.

9

SUMMARY AND IMPLICATIONS

For the better part of the current century, drug abuse in the United States has been typically described as a phenomenon characteristic of persons and groups only marginal to the general population and basic social order. A large segment of the literature has focused, for example, on narcotic addiction as it emerges within deviant groups (Coodley 1961; Cushman 1971; Inciardi 1972; Inciardi and Chambers 1972; Kolb 1925; Morgan 1965; Stanton 1969; Winick 1959-60), while an equally significant portion has concentrated on the problem as it exists within minority populations (Ball and Lau 1966; Chambers, Cuskey, and Moffett 1970; Chambers, Moffett, and Jones 1968; Klein and Phillips 1968). In addition, there is a vast body of literature describing drug users within the formal drug-treatment delivery system (Ball 1965; Pescor 1938; Ball and Chambers 1970).

During the past decade, however, considerable attention has focused on nonnarcotic drug problems and mixed addictions in order to identify additional populations of users and addicts (Inciardi 1974a; Moffet and Chambers 1970). These studies have stressed the need to go beyond the single model of the heroin street-addiction pattern, to conceptualize the drug problem as a phenomenon which includes many different populations of users and addicts, not all of which come to the attention of official drug treatment or law enforcement agencies.

An overview of the medical literature suggests that the hospital emergency room has long been recognized as a setting where drug-related problems appear (see, for example, Annis and Smart 1973; Caranasos, Stewart, and Cuff 1974; Chapel 1973; Dewhurst and Hatrick 1972; Done 1972), but the overwhelming portion of this literature has focused on the medical problems associated with overdose, suicide attempts, psychiatric disorders, addiction symptoms, and panic reactions (see Ladner, Russe, and Weppner 1975). Consequently, very little work has been done on the emergency room as a location for identifying trends in drug abuse or as a mechanism for treatment intervention.

The Acute Drug Reactions Project was initiated in 1972 for the purpose of documenting the role of the hospital emergency room in the identification and treatment of drug abusers, and preliminary data from the study reflected the somewhat unique aspects of the emergency-room patient population (Chambers, Petersen, and Newman 1975; Petersen and Thomas 1972; Petersen and Chambers 1975). These analyses seemed to suggest that the emergency-room setting represented an excellent base for generating information on the epidemiological aspects of drug use within a community. Not only could such data suggest the changing nature of drug abuse within a community, but in addition, they could serve to describe the basic characteristics of the changing populations of users. And this could be done in terms of both the illicit substances as well as the legally manufactured and distributed drugs. Furthermore, if done on a nationwide basis, a cross section of the changing patterns of drug use might be generated.

With this in mind, an attempt was made to expand the Miami-based effort into a nationwide consortium. The polydrug projects funded by the National Institute on Drug Abuse (NIDA) in numerous cities were invited to join, but due to conceptual differences and funding difficulties, only Denver, Houston, and New York were able to join the consortium. Ultimately, however, Houston and New York could not fully participate in the project, leaving Denver to serve as no more than a comparative data base. However, although the idea of a nationwide consortium never fully emerged, the Miami segment of the project expanded its data collection efforts for the purpose of developing the largest possible epidemiological data base on acute drug reactions in a community. The result was current and longitudinal information on acute drug reactions and drug-related deaths which clearly reflected the changing patterns of drug use in the Miami community. The preceding eight chapters of this book, written after the project ended, document these patterns in more detail and, in addition, provide information on the impact of treatment intervention in an emergency-room setting. The major findings of the project are summarized below, followed by a discussion of the implications of this study.

TRENDS IN DRUG EMERGENCIES

A major focus throughout the life of the project was the epidemiological one and this book serves to document the large size and changing nature of the drug problems and populations that come to the attention of the hospital emergency room. Data collection efforts were based at the emergency room of Jackson Memorial Hospital in Miami, which handled some 11,287 drug-emergency patients between January 1, 1972 and December 31, 1976. While previous studies indicate that the vast majority of drug-abuse patients in treatment programs are typically males and members of minority groups (Ball and Chambers 1970), the patient population in this effort was more often white (56.7 percent) and female (53.2 percent). Furthermore, the substances involved in the emergency-room treatment were most often legally manufactured and distributed drugs, rather than heroin and the other street drugs more typically involved for drug-program clients.

A focused analysis of these 11,287 drug emergency-room patients indicated that the population was changing and that the nature of drug emergencies was also changing. During the five-year study period, for example, it was found:

□ Drug emergencies involving barbiturates, nonbarbiturate sedatives, and hallucinogens declined proportionately while emergencies related to major tranquilizers, cocaine, and marijuana increased.

□ Drug emergencies involving panic reactions increased significantly while those related to overdose and suicide attempts decreased.

□ Males accounted for increasing percentages of drug emergencies (from 43.2 percent in 1972 to 50.6 percent in 1976), most notably those involving major tranquilizers, minor tranquilizers, barbiturate and nonbarbiturate sedatives, and over-the-counter drugs.

□ Drug-emergency patients became more concentrated in the 25-to-34 age category (going from 22.0 percent to 31.4 percent).

□ Overall, whites accounted for slightly decreasing percentages of drug-emergency patients (from 61.5 percent to 56.4 percent), with a corresponding increase among Hispanics (from 4.9 percent to 10.3 percent).

□ Hispanics represented increased percentages of drug emergencies involving both licit and illicit drugs, most notably prescription central-nervous-system depressants (from 5.7 percent to 13.6 percent), heroin (2.4 percent to 5.4 percent), and hallucinogens (3.2 percent to 9.0 percent).

□ The average age of drug patients seen for reactions to illegal drugs increased noticeably, particularly for heroin (21.5 to 24.0) and hallucinogens (18.8 to 21.4).

▢ Females accounted for a significantly greater percentage of marijuana emergencies (11.1 percent in 1972, 34.9 percent in 1976), although they represented a decreasing percentage of all other drug categories.

Chapter 2 contains the full discussion of these and related trends.

SUBPOPULATIONS AMONG EMERGENCY-ROOM DRUG PATIENTS

A comparison of the Jackson Memorial Hospital emergency-room data just discussed with those of other Dade County hospitals indicates that most Dade County emergencies involving street drugs are handled by Jackson Memorial, the one public hospital for the county. The major drug-emergency population at the private hospitals is thus much less diversified and consists primarily of white medicine misusers, particularly females. Details of and reasons for these differences are discussed in Chapter 3.

Extensive interviews with samples of emergency-room patients at both Jackson Memorial and Denver General Hospital provided more detailed information on social, drug-use, and crime-related characteristics of the drug patients. As reported in Chapter 4, it was found that these individuals tended to live in some arrangement other than that of married-living-with-spouse; have no more than a high-school education and in many cases not even this much formal certification; receive some kind of public assistance or with a recent history of such assistance; be unemployed at the time of the drug emergency; and be of blue-collar status, most commonly at the lower (unskilled) levels.

Inquiry into drug-use histories and contact with official community agencies suggested, further, that most of these patients could be characterized as falling into one of three subpopulations of drug cases. At one end of a continuum were minor-tranquilizer cases, who were typically white, female, and between ages 18 and 35, although males and Hispanics (but not blacks) also accounted for significant numbers of these patients. Most used minor tranquilizers on a regular basis, had begun using the drugs prior to age 25, were obtaining them legally, and had been using them in excess of two months. These individuals had only minimal involvement with other drugs, and they had rarely received any drug treatment; but about half of them had arrest records. At the other extreme were narcotics cases, who were typically male minority group members between the ages of 25 and 34. These individuals were, to an overwhelming degree, daily users of heroin who had begun using this drug prior to age 25. They were heavily involved with other drugs; 86 percent had arrest histories, and a significant portion had never received any drug-abuse treatment. Finally, emerging as a cross section of the tranquilizer and narcotics cases were sedative cases. These three subpopulations are discussed in detail in Chapter 4.

EMERGENCY MEDICAL TREATMENT
VERSUS DRUG-PROGRAM ENTRY

In order to better understand why so few drug-emergency patients reported experience with drug-abuse treatment programs, the Jackson Memorial drug-emergency patients were also compared with a population of clients in Dade County drug treatment programs. It was concluded that the many differences between these two populations could be traced fairly directly to the difference in the type of drug involved for the majority of each population. Specifically, the difference was one of licit drugs (especially tranquilizers and sedatives) being involved in drug emergencies versus illicit drugs (especially heroin) being involved for drug-program clients. More important than the difference in drug problem per se, however, was the consequent difference in social characteristics of the two populations in question. The primarily young, male, black, lower-status program clients contrasted strongly with the older, more-often white, and more-often female emergency patients. These social differences would seem to be more serious than the drug differences in making entry of medicine misusers into drug programs difficult to achieve. Details of the differences between the two populations are contained in Chapter 5, as is the discussion of the implications of these differences for the delivery of drug-abuse treatment services.

ALCOHOL-RELATED EMERGENCIES

We found that Jackson Memorial Hospital handles even more emergencies related to alcohol than other drug emergencies. In the 18 months following July 1, 1975, the Jackson Memorial emergency room admitted 5,004 alcohol-related cases, compared to 4,054 cases involving other substances. Compared to the drug patients, the alcohol patients tended to be considerably older (60 percent were over 35, compared to 21 percent of the drug patients) and more exclusively male (73 percent versus 50 percent).

As with the drug patients, detailed interviews were done with samples of these patients at both Jackson Memorial and Denver

General Hospital. The results indicated that the alcohol patients
tended to have even less education and even lower-status occupational
backgrounds than the drug patients. The two groups were also different with respect to drug-use history, in that the alcohol patients
were less likely to have ever used—and considerably less likely to
be currently using—drugs other than the substance which brought
them to the emergency room. Further, the alcohol patients were
more likely to have been arrested, and to have been arrested numerous times, than the other patients. In general, then, the older ages
and lower status, the relatively exclusive focus on use of alcohol,
and the heavier criminal-justice system involvement of the alcohol
patients suggest that a considerable number of them are typical of a
skid row population. The detailed findings concerning the alcohol
patients, particularly as they compare to the drug patients, are
provided in Chapter 6.

INTERVENTION AND REFERRAL

One of the major aims of the Acute Drug Reactions Project was
to provide intervention services to that population of drug users who
came to the attention of hospital emergency rooms for acute or adverse reactions to drugs. This idea was based on data which indicated that the Jackson Memorial Hospital emergency room in Dade
County, Florida provided emergency treatment to an excess of 1,000
patients per year, but that these patients were not provided any post-
emergency or posthospital services relative to their recent drug
experience. It was hypothesized that if patients were offered therapeutic intervention during a drug-related crisis, such intervention
might serve to prevent future drug crises, or at least diminish the
extent of the user's poshospital drug-taking behavior.
During the early years of the research, project personnel offered intervention counseling to a variety of patient cohorts, referred
the patients to various components of the local Dade County human-
services delivery network, and conducted field followup studies. In
general, five significant findings emerged from the effort.
First, it was determined that intervention in the emergency-
room setting had benefits in initiating treatment contact. It had been
standard procedure at the hospital for emergency-room physicians
to refer heroin patients to local drug treatment programs before the
beginning of the Acute Drug Reactions Project, but a followup on a
portion of these heroin referrals found that the procedure was not
overwhelmingly fruitful—only 38.6 percent had ever made treatment
contact. By contrast, among those cases counseled and referred by
project staff, 66.7 percent ultimately made treatment contact.

Second, although the findings were based on small samples, it was suggested by the followup that the greater the contacts made with patients by project staff, the greater were the chances that the individual would discontinue drug use. Among those patient groups with whom there was no contact prior to followup, 44 percent to 55 percent later reported no further drug use; among those with whom there was contact, reported discontinuance ranged from 60 percent to 94 percent.

Third, the success of any patient followup depends largely on the nature and extent of intake data collected on patients' friends and relatives. Of the patients referred to treatment by project staff, as many as 45 percent could not be located, primarily as the result of patient mobility patterns. That is, of those who could not be located in the field, 77 percent had simply moved and left no forwarding addresses, and the necessary information for learning their whereabouts through parents, friends, or relatives had not been collected. This cohort of unreachable respondents, furthermore, were found to be primarily white females under age 35 who were users of illicit substances.

Fourth, a major difficulty circumscribed the actual placement of drug users in those social service agencies which were not considered traditional drug treatment programs. These "nondrug" agencies appeared unwilling to deal with drug-using clients even when the patient's problem was understood to be of a "nondrug" nature, and the programs would ultimately rerefer the case to a local drug-abuse treatment program.

Fifth, and importantly, it was found that a major portion of the patients in the emergency-room setting were abusers of legally manufactured and distributed drugs, and significant here was the high incidence of medicine misusers. These medicine misusers were persons involved in self-medication with prescription tranquilizers and sedatives, and over-the-counter drugs, and were not associated in any way with the lifestyle and drug-taking and drug-seeking behaviors of active street drug abusers. And while these persons indeed had a drug problem, there were no services in the community geared to deal with their substance-abuse situation.

The background history, procedures, and specific findings for the intervention and referral phase of the project are discussed in Chapter 7.

DRUG-RELATED DEATHS

Finally, as an additional means of expanding the epidemiological data base accumulated by the Acute Drug Reactions Project, 20 years' worth of Dade County Medical Examiner records were examined. Information was gathered on both suicides and accidental deaths for 1956 through 1975. The results support several of the findings of other parts of the project, notably (1) a decline, over time, in the proportion of drug emergencies attributable to barbiturates; (2) the involvement of a broader spectrum of population subgroups in drug emergencies related to tranquilizers and sedatives—specifically, more males, more young people, and more Hispanics, rather than the almost exclusive involvement of white females over age 25; and, most importantly (3) the position of prescription central-nervous-system depressants—sedatives and tranquilizers—as the number-one drug danger, even in a community with unusually high rates of illicit-drug use. Also of interest in the drug-death information are trends concerning changing levels of heroin use; the heroin epidemic of the late 1960s seems clearly identified in these data, including specification of the social groups most affected by it. The details of this part of the project, summarized by drug type and by five-year period, are given in Chapter 8.

IMPLICATIONS

There are a variety of implications in these data, the most prominent of which can be listed as follows:

- The hospital emergency room represents a primary mechanism for treatment intervention for drug abusers.
- Intervention in the emergency-room setting appears as an effective technique for initiating treatment.
- As a research endeavor, emergency-room data can examine trends in drug use and isolate the fads and fashions in drug use over time.
- Emergency-room data reflect the existence of drug-using populations not known to the criminal justice system or the human-services delivery network.
- Most importantly, emergency-room data indicate the existence of a large population of medicine misusers for whom no treatment services are available in the community.

APPENDIX:

DATA COLLECTION FORMS

NATIONAL CENTER FOR THE STUDY
OF ACUTE DRUG REACTIONS

Hospital Data Form (Form A)

Patient name _____

Patient address_____

Patient JMH no. _____

Age _____ Sex: 1. Male   Race: 1. Black
                2. Female   2. Spanish
                                       3. White

Date_____

Time _____

Admit 1. Emergency room   Transfer_____
      2. Ward
      3. Crisis

Principal Substance _____
Secondary Substance (ETOH* first)_____
Third Substance _____
Fourth Substance _____

Complaint at Admission _____
    01. suicide attempt   10. panic reactions
    02. overdose   11. psychiatric evaluation
    03. allergic reaction   12. public intoxication
    04. withdrawal   13. extrapyramidal effects
    05. physical addiction   14. ETOH seizures
    06. infections, localized   15. DT's
    07. systemic infections   16. cirrhosis, GI problems
        (hepatitis, endocarditis) 17. other, specify _____
    08. psychotic reactions

Clinical Status_____
    1. conscious and coherent   3. unconscious
    2. conscious and incoherent 4. dead

Disposition _____
    1. left without treatment   5. treated, admitted to
    2. treated and released   psychiatric ward
    3. treated, left against   6. treated, admitted medical ward
       medical advice   7. treated and jailed
    4. treated, referred   8. dead
       (specify)_____

Psychiatric Diagnosis _____

Coder identification _____

_____

    *Alcohol

161

National Emergency Room Survey (Form B)

1. City: 1. Miami   3. Denver
       2. New York   4. Houston

2. Hospital _____

3. Hospital Type: 1. Public
                 2. Private
                 3. Voluntary (Proprietary)

4. Hospital Referral Unit:
    1. Medical Emergency Room
    2. Psychiatric Emergency Room
    3. Jail ward (security ward)
    4. Other hospital ward
    5. Outpatient department
    9. No data

5. Name of Respondent:
(Last, first, M.I.)

6. Address:
Number _____
Street   _____
         _____
City   _____
State   _____
Phone number _____
Apt. No. _____
Nearest Intersection _____
Zip Code _____

7. Person locally who can be contacted:
Name _____
Address _____
       _____
Relationship _____
Phone _____

8. Date of Birth:

_____ / _____ / _____
month   / day / year

9. Sex:
1. Male   2. Female

10. Ethnicity:
    01. White
    02. Black
    03. American Indian
    04. Oriental
    05. Puerto Rican
    06. Mexican American
    07. Cuban
    08. Other Hispanic
    09. Other (specify)
    _____
    99. No data

11. Marital Status:
    1. Never married
    2. Common law
    3. Married
    4. Separated
    5. Divorced
    6. Widowed
    9. No data

12. Living Arrangement:
    1. Alone
    2. Spouse
    3. Parents
    4. Other relatives
    5. Friends
    6. Institution
    7. Children
    8. Other (specify)
    _____
    9. No data

13. Education:
    Years of school _____
    Highest diploma or degree held:
    1. None
    2. Grade school
    3. High school
    4. G.E.D.
    5. Post-high school
       vocational or educational
    6. Junior college
    7. College
    8. Graduate degree
    9. No data

14. Occupation:
    Present _____
    Usual _____

    01. Professional-technical
    02. Manager-administrative
    03. Sales
    04. Clerical office worker
    05. Skilled craftsman
    06. Semi-skilled operator
    07. Unskilled worker
    08. Service worker
    10. Housewife
    11. Student
    12. Unemployed
    13. Other (specify)
    _____
    9. No data

    If respondent is a student:
    1. Enrolled and attending
    2. Enrolled, not attending

15. Employment Status:
    1. Full-time (30 hours a week or more)
    2. Part-time (less than 30 hours a week)
    3. Currently unemployed
    9. No data

16. Number of months on present job?_____

17. Number of months employed during the last two years?_____

18. Public Assistance:
    1. Never received
    2. Currently receiving
    3. Not currently receiving, but has applied

    4. Received but not within past 2 years
    5. Received within past 2 years but not currently receiving
    9. No data

    If currently receiving, ask source:
    1. Welfare
    2. Unemployment
    3. VA

    4. Social Security
    5. Other (specify)_____
    9. No data

ARREST HISTORY

19. Have you ever been arrested?
    1. Yes   2. No

20. If yes, age at first arrest _____

21. List all arrest offenses: (except juvenile)

    _____   _____
    _____   _____
    _____   _____
    _____   _____
    _____   _____

    a) total arrests _____
    b) total convictions _____
    c) total drug crimes _____
    d) total property crimes* _____
    e) total personal crimes† _____
    f) total arrests during last two years _____

    _____

    *Property crimes include: burglary, breaking and entering, larceny, auto theft, buying-receiving-possessing stolen property
    †Personal crimes include: homicide, forcible rape, assault, robbery.

Substance Use History

22. Have you ever been in treatment for drug or alcohol use?
    (Number of months for drugs in columns 11 and 12; alcohol
    in columns 14 and 15)
    1. No
    2. Yes, previously (if yes, how many months since treatment?)
    3. Yes, currently (if yes, how many months have you been in
       treatment?)
    4. Both 2 and 3 (if both, number of months in treatment)
    9. No data

23. How many separate times have you been in a treatment pro-
    gram for drug use during the past two years?

    Alcohol use?

    _____(0-8)   _____(0-8)

24. What types of treatment have you had, and how often? (Up to 8)

		Drugs	Alcohol	Non-substance related
a.	Residential facility			
b.	Methadone Maintenance			
c.	Antagonist			
d.	Public inpatient psychiatric facility			
e.	Private (or voluntary) inpatient psychiatric facility			
f.	OPD psychiatric			
g.	Detoxification (inpatient)			
h.	Detoxification (outpatient)			
i.	Other inpatient (specify)			
j.	Community mental health center			
k.	Daycare			
l.	Private therapy			
m.	Other (specify)			

25. Admission type (Drugs and Alcohol-last 2 years)
    1. New admission
    2. Readmission (column 57 drug, 60 alcohol)
       (Note: If drug readmission, record in Col. 58 the number
       of readmissions to this hospital and in Col. 59 the total
       number to any hospital. If alcohol readmission, record in
       Col. 61 the number of readmissions to this hospital and in
       Col. 62 the total number to any hospital; up to 8 readmis-
       sions and admissions).

26. Drugs Ever Used:

Drug	First Use		Current Use		
	Age	Year	Frequency	Doses per day	Cost
01. Heroin					
02. Methadone					
03. Other narcotics					
04. Barbiturates					
05. Other sedatives					
06. Minor tranquilizers					
07. Major tranquilizers					
08. Anti-depressants					
09. Cocaine					
10. Amphetamines					
11. Other stimulants					
12. Analgesics					
13. Marijuana/hashish					
14. LSD					
15. Other psychotogens					
16. Solvents/inhalants					
17. Other (specify)					

Frequency Codes:
1. Daily
2. Several times/week
3. Once a week
4. Every two weeks
5. Less than once/month
6. Does not use
9. No data

	27	28
	Primary Substance Responsible for Admittance	Secondary Substance Responsible for Admittance
Drug		
Length of Use (in months)		
Frequency (same categories as Question 26)		
Doses per Day		
Age, first Use		
How Obtained		

	29	30	31
	Current Major Drug of Abuse	Current Secondary Drug of Abuse	Drug of Choice
Drug			
Length of Use (in months)			
Frequency (same categories as Question 26)			
Doses per Day			
Age, first Use			
How Obtained			

Frequency Codes:
1. Daily
2. Several times/week
3. Once a week
4. Every two weeks
5. Less than once/month
6. Does not use
9. No data

Codes for how obtained
1. Prescription, legitimate (own)
2. Prescription, legitimate (someone else's)
3. Prescription, illegal
4. OTC drug
5. Street
6. Jail
7. Physician hopping
8. Other (specify) _____
9. No data

Q. F. V. Alcohol Index

Alcohol Use (last 2 years)

32. About how often do you usually drink any kind of beverages which have alcohol in them? (If "every day," ASK HOW MANY TIMES A DAY).

3 or more times a day----------------------------------01
2 times a day---------------------------------------02
once a day--- 03
nearly every day------------------------------------04
3 or 4 times a week--------------------------------- 05
once or twice a week-------------------------------- 06
2 or 3 times a month-------------------------------- 07
about once a month----------------------------------08
less than once a month ----------------------------09
less than once a year, not sure----------------------10
does not drink alcoholic beverages------------------11
no data-- 99

33. About how often do you usually drink wine?

3 or more times a day----------------------------------01
2 times a day---------------------------------------02
once a day--- 03
nearly every day------------------------------------04
3 or 4 times a week--------------------------------- 05
once or twice a week-------------------------------- 06
2 or 3 times a month-------------------------------- 07
about once a month----------------------------------08
less than once a month----------------------------- 09
less than once a year, not sure----------------------10
does not drink wine-------------------------------- 11
no data--99

34. Please think about all the times you have had wine recently. Which numbered position on this card (HAND RESPONDENT CARD) comes closest to how often you have as many as five or six glasses at one time?

nearly every time---------------------------------- 1
more than half the time---------------------------- 2
less than half the time---------------------------- 3
once in a while------------------------------------ 4
never, not sure------------------------------------ 5
no data-- 9

35. Which position on the card is closest to how often you have three or four glasses when you drink wine?

    nearly every time------------------------------------ 1
    more than half the time----------------------------- 2
    less than half the time------------------------------ 3
    once in a while-------------------------------------- 4
    never, not sure-------------------------------------- 5
    no data-- 9

36. Which position on the card is closest to how often you have one or two glasses when you drink wine?

    nearly every time------------------------------------ 1
    more than half the time----------------------------- 2
    less than half the time------------------------------ 3
    once in a while-------------------------------------- 4
    never, not sure-------------------------------------- 5
    no data-- 9

37. Switching to beer, about how often do you usually drink beer?

    3 or more times a day-------------------------------- 01
    2 times a day-- 02
    once a day--- 03
    nearly every day------------------------------------- 04
    3 or 4 times a week---------------------------------- 05
    once or twice a week--------------------------------- 06
    2 or 3 times a month--------------------------------- 07
    about once a month----------------------------------- 08
    less than once a month------------------------------- 09
    less than once a year, not sure---------------------- 10
    does not drink beer---------------------------------- 11
    no data-- 99

38. Thinking about all the times you have had beer recently, which position on the card (HAND RESPONDENT CARD, YELLOW) comes closest to how often you have had as many as five or six cans or bottles?

    nearly every time------------------------------------ 1
    more than half the time----------------------------- 2
    less than half the time------------------------------ 3
    once in a while-------------------------------------- 4
    never, not sure-------------------------------------- 5
    no data-- 9

39. How often do you usually have three or four cans or bottles of beer?

   nearly every time-- 1
   more than half the time----------------------------------- 2
   less than half the time------------------------------------ 3
   once in a while-- 4
   never, not sure-- 5
   no data-- 9

40. How often do you have one or two bottles or cans of beer?

   nearly every time-- 1
   more than half the time----------------------------------- 2
   less than half the time------------------------------------ 3
   once in a while-- 4
   never, not sure-- 5
   no data-- 9

41. Switching to drinks containing whiskey, or cocktails mixed with hard liquor, about how often do you usually have drinks of this kind?

   3 or more times a day-------------------------------------- 01
   2 times a day-- 02
   once a day--- 03
   nearly every day--- 04
   3 or 4 times a week-- 05
   once or twice a week--------------------------------------- 06
   2 or 3 times a month--------------------------------------- 07
   about once a month--- 08
   less than once a month------------------------------------- 09
   less than once a year, not sure--------------------------- 10
   does not drink hard liquor-------------------------------- 11
   no data-- 99

42. Thinking about all the times you have had hard liquor or cocktails recently, which position on the card (HAND RESPONDENT CARD) comes closest to how often you have as many as five or six drinks?

   nearly every time-- 1
   more than half the time----------------------------------- 2
   less than half the time------------------------------------ 3
   once in a while-- 4
   never, not sure-- 5
   no data-- 9

43. How often do you usually have three or four drinks?

nearly every time--- 1
more than half the time----------------------------------- 2
less than half the time----------------------------------- 3
once in a while--- 4
never, not sure--- 5
no data-- 9

44. How often do you usually have one or two drinks?

nearly every time--- 1
more than half the time----------------------------------- 2
less than half the time----------------------------------- 3
once in a while--- 4
never, not sure--- 5
no data-- 9

45. (ASK ALL DRINKERS)
Which alcoholic beverage do you drink most frequently--beer,
wine or hard liquor?

beer-- 1
wine-- 2
hard liquor-- 3
no data-- 9

46. Do you use any non-beverage alcohol?

yes--- 1
no-- 2
tried, but not currently using--------------------------- 3
no data-- 9

47. How old were you when you first began drinking any type of
alcoholic beverage?

_____

48. Respondent's alcohol classification (for ALL respondents)

heavy drinker-- 1
moderate drinker--- 2
light drinker-- 3
infrequent drinker--------------------------------------- 4
abstainer-- 5
no data-- 9

49.   What was the reason for your coming to the hospital?

    01 suicide attempt
    02 overdose
    03 allergic reaction
    04 withdrawal
    05 physical addiction
    06 infections, localized
    07 systemic infections (including hepatitis, endocarditis, etc.
    08 psychotic reactions
    09 panic reactions
    10 psychiatric evaluation
    11 public intoxication
    12 extrapyramidal reactions
    13 seizures
    14 delirium tremens (DT's)
    15 cirrhosis, G.I. problems
    16 other, specify _____

    _____
    _____

    99 no data

50.   Coder Identification Number

Medical Examiner Survey   (Form C)
(Suicides/Overdose Deaths)

1. Case Number

2. Nature of death: 1. accident 2. suicide

3. Nature of suicide: 01. barbiturate
                              02. other drug/chemical (not poison)
                              03. plastic bags
                              04. fire
                              05. hanging
                              06. gunshot
                              07. drowning
                              08. stabbing/laceration
                              09. jumping
                              10. carbon monoxide
                              11. poison (e.g. arsenic)
                              12-98. other: _____

4. Suicide pact: 1. Yes.   2. No   3. Suicide/homicide

5. Sex: 1. Male   2. Female

6. Date of death

7. Substance causing death
   a) _____
   b) _____
   c) _____

8. Race: 1. white
          2. black
          3. Spanish
          4. Oriental
          5. American Indian
          6. other (specify)

9. Age: _____

10. Address where death occurred _____

_____

11. Suicide in jail? 1. Yes   2. No

12. City where death occurred: _____

13. State of birth (if not in U.S.A., name country)
SP-Spain   CB-Cuba   PR-Puerto Rico
BH-Bahama   OS-Other Spanish
YY-all other countries: _____

14. Married:
    1. common law
    2. married
    3. divorced
    4. separated
    5. widowed
    6. never married

15. Surviving spouse: 1. Yes 2. No

16. Usual occupation _____
    01. professional-technical
    02. manager-administrative
    03. sales
    04. clerical office worker
    05. skilled craftsman
    06. semi-skilled operator
    07. unskilled worker
    08. service worker
    10. housewife
    11. student
    12. unemployed
    13. other (specify)
    99. no data

17. Alcoholic content

18. State of residence _____

19. City of residence _____

20. Address of residence _____

21. Special incident codes:
    (see code sheets)

22. Special place codes:
    (see code sheets)

REFERENCES

Adams, Kenneth M., Phillip M. Rennick, Kenneth G. Schoof, and John F. Keegan. 1975. "Neuropsychological Measurement of Drug Effects: Polydrug Research." Journal of Psychedelic Drugs 7 (2): 151-60.

Annis, H., and R. Smart. 1973. "Adverse Reactions and Recurrences from Marihuana Use." British Journal of the Addictions 68: 315-19.

Ball, John C. 1965. "Two Patterns of Narcotic Addiction in the United States." Journal of Criminal Law, Criminology and Police Science 56 (June): 203-11.

Ball, John C., and Carl D. Chambers, eds. 1970. The Epidemiology of Opiate Addiction in the United States. Springfield, Ill.: Charles C. Thomas.

Ball, John C., and M. P. Lau. 1966. "The Chinese Narcotic Addict in the United States." Social Forces 45 (September): 68-72.

Benvenuto, John, and Peter G. Bourne. 1975. "The Federal Polydrug Abuse Project: Initial Report." Journal of Psychedelic Drugs 7 (2): 115-20.

Berger, F. M. 1967. "Drugs and Suicide in the United States." Clinical Pharmacology and Therapeutics 8 (2): 219-23.

Berman, J. I., and E. Luck. 1971. "Patients' Ethnic Backgrounds Affect Utilization: Reporting of a Study of Emergency Services." Hospitals 45 (14): 64-68.

Blair, Lewis H., and John Sessler. 1974. Drug Program Assessment: A Community Guide. Washington, D.C.: Drug Abuse Council.

Cahalan, Don, Ira H. Cisin, and Helen M. Crossley. 1969. American Drinking Practices: A National Study of Drinking Behavior and Attitudes. New Brunswick, N.J.: Rutgers Center of Alcohol Studies.

175

Caranasos, George J., Ronald B. Stewart, and Leighton E. Cuff. 1974. "Drug-Induced Illness Leading to Hospitalization." Journal of the American Medical Association 228 (May 6): 713-17.

Chambers, Carl D., Walter R. Cuskey, and Arthur D. Moffett. 1970. "Demographic Factors in Opiate Addiction Among Mexican-Americans." Public Health Reports 85 (June): 523-31.

Chambers, Carl D., James A. Inciardi, and Harvey A. Siegal, eds. 1975. Chemical Coping: A Report on Legal Drug Use in the United States. New York: Spectrum Publications.

Chambers, Carl D., Arthur D. Moffett, and Judith P. Jones. 1968. "Demographic Factors Associated with Negro Opiate Addiction." International Journal of the Addictions 3 (Fall): 329-43.

Chambers, Carl D., David M. Petersen, and S. C. Newman. 1975. "Acute Drug Reactions in a Hospital Emergency Room—A Demographic and Social Assessment." Journal of the Florida Medical Association 62 (May): 40-42.

Chapel, James L. 1973. "Emergency Room Treatment of the Drug Abusing Patient." American Journal of Psychiatry 130 (3): 257-59.

Cherubin, C. F., J. McKusker, M. Baden, F. Kavaler, and Z. O. Amsel. 1972. "The Epidemiology of Death in Narcotic Addicts." American Journal of Epidemiology 96 (1): 11-22.

Coodley, A. E. 1961. "Current Aspects of Delinquency and Addiction." Archives of General Psychiatry 4 (June): 632-40.

Cushman, Peter. 1971. "Methadone Maintenance in Hard-Core Criminal Addicts: Economic Effects." New York State Journal of Medicine 71 (July 15): 1768-74.

Dewhurst, K., and J. Hatrick. 1972. "Differential Diagnosis and Treatment of LSD-Induced Psychosis." Practitioner 209 (September): 327-32.

Done, A. 1972. "What To Do Until the Patient Wakes Up." Emergency Medicine 4 (9): 176-78.

Douglas, Jack D. 1967. The Social Meaning of Suicide. Princeton: Princeton University Press.

Dublin, Louis I. 1963. Suicide: A Sociological and Statistical Study. New York: Ronald Press.

Duff, Raymond S., and August Hollingshead. 1968. Sickness and Society. New York: Harper and Row.

DuPont, Robert L. 1974. "Amid the Bureaucratic Maze, SAODAP Boss Plots U.S. Thrust." The Journal of the Addiction Research Foundation (Toronto), April 1.

DuPont, Robert L., and Mark H. Greene. 1973. "The Dynamics of a Heroin Addiction Epidemic." Science 181 (August 24): 716-22.

Fallding, Harold, and Carol Miles. 1974. Drinking, Community and Civilization; The Account of a New Jersey Interview Study. New Brunswick, N.J.: Rutgers Center of Alcohol Studies.

Freed, E. X. 1973. "Drug Abuse by Alcoholics: A Review." International Journal of the Addictions 8: 451-73.

Freedman, Alfred M., and Richard E. Brotman. 1969. "Multiple Drug Use Among Teenagers: Plans for Action and Research." In Drugs and Youth, edited by J. R. Wittenborn, H. Brilly, J. P. Smith, and S. A. Wittenborn, pp. 335-44. Springfield, Ill.: Charles C. Thomas.

Glasscote, R. M., J. N. Sussex, J. H. Jaffe, J. Ball, and L. Brill. 1972. The Treatment of Drug Abuse: Programs, Problems, Prospects. Washington, D.C.: Joint Information Service of the American Psychiatric Association and the National Association for Mental Health.

Goodwin, Donald W. 1973. "Alcohol in Suicide and Homicide." Quarterly Journal of Studies on Alcohol 34 (A): 144-56.

Inciardi, James A. 1974a. "Drugs, Drug-Taking, and Drug-Seeking: Notations on the Dynamics of Myth, Change, and Reality." In Drugs and the Criminal Justice System, edited by James A. Inciardi and Carl D. Chambers, pp. 203-30. Beverly Hills, Calif.: Sage.

_____. 1974b. "The Villification of Euphoria: Some Perspectives on an Elusive Issue." Addictive Diseases 1: 241-67.

_____. 1972. "Patterns of Drug Use Among Village Beats: A Research Note." International Journal of the Addictions 7 (4): 649-53.

Inciardi, James A., and Carl D. Chambers. 1972. "Unreported Criminal Involvement of Narcotic Addicts." Journal of Drug Issues 2 (Spring): 57-64.

Inciardi, James A., Duane C. McBride, and Anne E. Pottieger. 1978. "Gambling with Death: Some Theoretical and Empirical Considerations on Drugs and Suicide." In When Coping Strategies Fail, edited by Dan J. Lettieri. Beverly Hills, Calif.: Sage.

Inciardi, James A., David M. Petersen, and Carl D. Chambers. 1974. "Methaqualone Abuse Patterns, Diversion Paths and Adverse Reactions." Journal of the Florida Medical Association 61 (April).

Judd, Lewis L., and Igor Grant. 1975. "Brain Dysfunction in Chronic Sedative Users." Journal of Psychedelic Drugs 7 (2): 143-50.

Kirby, Michael W., and G. James Berry. 1975. "Selected Descriptive Characteristics of Polydrug Abusers." Journal of Psychedelic Drugs 7 (2): 161-67.

Klein, Julius, and Derek L. Phillips. 1968. "From Hard to Soft Drugs: Temporal and Substantive Changes in Drug Usage Among Gangs in a Working-Class Community." Journal of Health and Social Behavior 9 (June): 139-45.

Kolb, L. 1925. "Drug Addiction in Its Relation to Crime." Mental Hygiene 9 (January): 74-89.

Kunnes, Richard. 1973. "Poly-Drug Abuse: Drug Companies and Doctors." American Journal of Orthopsychiatry 43 (July): 530-32.

Ladner, Robert A., Brian R. Russe, and Robert S. Weppner. 1975. "Acute and Chronic Drug Problems Responsible for Emergency Hospital Admissions: A Preliminary Analysis of Complaint, Drug and Response." Journal of Psychedelic Drugs 7 (2): 215-28.

Lewis, J. M. 1973. "The Multiple Drug User." Texas Medicine 69 (October): 59-62.

Mayfield, D. G., and D. Montgomery. 1972. "Alcoholism, Alcohol Intoxication, and Suicide Attempts." Archives of General Psychiatry 27: 349-53.

McGrath, John H., and Frank R. Scarpitti, eds. 1967. Youth and Drugs. Glenview, Ill.: Scott, Foresman.

Moffett, Arthur D., and Carl D. Chambers. 1970. "The Hidden Addiction." Social Work 15 (July): 54-59.

Morgan, J. P., Jr. 1965. "Drug Addiction: Criminal or Medical Problem?" Police (July-August): 6-9.

Murray, Robin N. 1977. "Screening and Early Detection Instruments for Disabilities Related to Alcohol Consumption." In Alcohol-Related Disabilities, edited by G. Edwards, M. M. Gross, M. Keller, J. Moser, and R. Room, pp. 89-106. Geneva: World Health Organization (Offset Pub. No. 32).

National Institute on Alcohol Abuse and Alcoholism (NIAAA). 1975. Proceedings: Seminar on Public Health Services and the Public Inebriate. Washington, D.C.: Government Printing Office (DHEW Pub. No. [ADM] 75-218).

_____. 1974. Alcohol and Health: New Knowledge. 2d Special Report to the U.S. Congress, from the Secretary of Health, Education and Welfare, June. Washington, D.C.: U.S. Government Printing Office (DHEW Pub. No. [ADM] 75-212).

Pescor, M. J. 1938. "A Statistical Analysis of the Clinical Records of Hospitalized Drug Addicts." Public Health Reports, Supplement No. 143: 1-23.

Petersen, David M., and Carl D. Chambers. 1975. "Demographic Characteristics of Emergency Room Admissions for Acute Drug Reactions." International Journal of the Addictions 10 (6): 963-75.

Petersen, David M., and Charles W. Thomas. 1975. "Acute Drug Reactions Among the Elderly." Journal of Gerontology 30 (5): 552-56.

Pittman, David J., and C. Wayne Gordon. 1958. Revolving Door: A Study of the Chronic Police Case Inebriate. Glencoe, Ill.: Free Press.

Project DAWN III. 1976. Drug Abuse Warning Network, Phase III Report. Washington, D.C.: Drug Enforcement Administration and National Institute on Drug Abuse.

Raynes, Anthony E., Vernon D. Patch, and Miriam Cohen. 1975. "Comparison of Opiate and Polydrug Abusers in Treatment." Journal of Psychedelic Drugs 7 (2): 135-42.

Setter, John G., John F. Maher, and George E. Schreiner. 1966. "Barbiturate Intoxication." Archives of Internal Medicine 117 (February): 224-36.

Stanton, John M. 1969. Lawbreaking and Drug Dependence. Albany: State of New York, Division of Parole, Bureau of Research and Statistics.

Weppner, Robert S., and Duane C. McBride. 1975. "Comprehensive Drug Programs: The Dade County Example." American Journal of Psychiatry 132: 734-38.

_____, eds. 1974. Profile of the Metropolitan Dade County Comprehensive Drug Program and Its Affiliates. Miami: Dade County monograph.

Weppner, Robert S., Karen S. Wells, Duane C. McBride, and Robert A. Ladner. 1976. "Effects of Criminal Justice and Medical Definitions of a Social Problem Upon the Delivery of Treatment: The Case of Drug Abuse." Journal of Health and Social Behavior 17 (June): 170-77.

Wesson, Donald R., David E. Smith, and Steven E. Lerner. 1975. "Streetwise and Nonstreetwise Polydrug Typology: Myth or Reality." Journal of Psychedelic Drugs 7 (2): 121-34.

Winick, Charles. 1959-60. "The Use of Drugs by Jazz Musicians." Social Problems 7 (Winter): 240-53.

Wolfgang, Marvin E., and Rolf B. Strohm. 1956. "The Relationship Between Alcohol and Criminal Homicide." Quarterly Journal of Studies on Alcohol 17: 411-25.

INDEX

active versus passive intervention, 115, 117-23

Acute Drug Reactions Project (ADRP), 2-7, 152-58; alcohol related, 24, 83-84, 86-87, 88-89, 100-101; Dade County CDP data, 72; extended interviews, 34-36; Medical Examiner data, 131-32; private hospital data, 26; referral and intervention, 1-3, 111-30, 156-57, 158 (see also Denver, Jackson Memorial Hospital)

Adams, Kenneth M., 4

adverse reactions (see alcohol emergencies, drug emergencies)

age: of drug/alcohol users/patients, 4, 9-12, 21, 27, 32, 35, 36, 40, 57-60, 70, 74, 82, 87-89, 90, 93, 97, 100, 107, 109, 114-15, 124, 127, 136-38, 141, 149-50, 153, 154-55, 156, 157, 158; at first arrest, 54, 105, 108; at first drug use, 48-51, 62-63, 78, 82, 154-55

alcohol: in American society, 83, 95-96, 97; versus drugs, 87; as a secondary substance in drug emergencies, 41, 52, 85, 93-94, 133 (see also alcohol emergencies, nonbeverage alcohol, Q-F-V index)

alcohol drownings, 132-33

alcohol emergencies, 24, 28, 83-110, 124-25; incidence, 24, 25, 86, 155; secondary-substance involvement, 93;

specific types, 84-86, 93-95, 100, 101-102, 132-33

alcoholism/alcoholics, 83-84, 86, 93, 104-105, 109 (see also heavy drinking, problem drinking)

amphetamines, 12, 46, 48, 63, 85, 136, 141, 148-49 (see also stimulants)

analgesics (prescription, non-narcotic), 33, 46, 63, 101, 125, 135, 136, 148-49

Annis, H., 151

antidepressants, 12, 33, 46, 51 (see also stimulants)

Ball, John C., 151

barbiturates, 12, 21, 40, 46, 51, 57, 63, 85, 98, 99, 101, 132, 135, 136, 150, 153, 158 (see also sedatives)

Benvenuto, John, 4

Berger, F. M., 132

Berman, J. I., 74

Berry, G. James, 4

Blair, Lewis H., 131

Bourne, Peter G., 4

Brotman, Richard E., 133

Cahalan, Don, 83, 96, 97

Caranasos, George J., 151

Chambers, Carl D., 83, 85, 86, 151, 152

Chapel, James L., 151

Cherubin, C. F., 131

Cisin, Ira H., 83, 96, 97

clinical status (including consciousness) at time of admission, 16, 28, 93

ABOUT THE AUTHORS

JAMES A. INCIARDI is Associate Professor and director of the Division of Criminal Justice, University of Delaware. He received his Ph.D. at New York University in 1973. Dr. Inciardi has some 14 years' experience in the clinical and research aspects of drug abuse, and was director of both the Acute Drug Reactions Project and the National Center for the Study of Acute Drug Reactions in 1975 and 1976. In addition, he is editor of Criminology, and has published more than 60 books and articles in the areas of drug abuse, criminology, and criminal justice.

DUANE C. McBRIDE is currently an Assistant Professor in the Department of Psychiatry, University of Miami School of Medicine, and serves as deputy director of the Department's Division of Addiction Sciences. He received his M.A. from the University of Maryland in 1970 and his Ph.D. from the University of Kentucky in 1976. Since 1973 he has been conducting research on the effectiveness of treatment services for drug users, with a particular emphasis on the linkage between drug users in the criminal justice system and community drug treatment programs. He is also author of numerous articles in professional journals.

ANNE E. POTTIEGER is a research associate in the Division of Criminal Justice at the University of Delaware. She received her Ph.D. in sociology at the University of Delaware in 1977. Dr. Pottieger is managing editor of Criminology and has published in the areas of suicide, violence, drug abuse, alcoholism, and criminological theory.

BRIAN R. RUSSE is a member of the research faculty of the Division of Addiction Sciences, Department of Psychiatry, University of Miami School of Medicine, and formerly associate director of the National Center for the Study of Acute Drug Reactions. Mr. Russe received his M.Ed. in psychology at the University of Miami in 1975, and has published widely in the areas of criminology and substance abuse.

HARVEY A. SIEGAL is Assistant Professor of Medical Sociology, School of Medicine, and Assistant Professor, Department of Sociology, Anthropology, and Social Work at Wright State University. He received his Ph.D. from Yale University and has worked in academic positions in both Miami and Mexico. He has coedited three books on drug addiction and crime and has authored <u>Outposts of the Forgotten: Lifeways of Socially Terminal People in Slum Hotels and Single Room Occupancy Tenements</u> (1978).

RELATED TITLES
Published by
Praeger Special Studies

ALIENATION IN CONTEMPORARY SOCIETY:
A Multidisciplinary Examination

> edited by
> Roy S. Bryce-Laporte
> Claudewell S. Thomas

DRUG USE AND ABUSE AMONG U.S. MINORITIES:
An Annotated Bibliography

> Patti Iiyama
> Setsuko Matsunaga Nishi
> Bruce D. Johnson

DRUGS, CRIME, AND POLITICS

> edited by
> Arnold S. Trebach